An APMP

MW00898884

A comprehensive guide to that part of the APM Body of Knowledge that pertains to the syllabus of the APMP examination.

Robin Kay BA MBA APMP

Copyright © 2009 by R.J.Kay.

robinjohnkay@aol.com

All rights reserved. No part of this publication may be reproduced, stored in a retrieval system, transmitted or utilised in any form or by any means, electronic, mechanical, photocopying, recording or otherwise without written permission from the author.

ISBN: 978-1-4092-6707-2

Preface

The information contained within this book is based upon sound and generally accepted project management principals. It is intended to cover those areas of the APM Body of Knowledge (5th edition, 2006) that are included in the APMP syllabus (3rd edition). Although the material in this book is based on the author's knowledge it is primarily driven by, and aligned with, the Body of Knowledge.

The APMP qualification is a knowledge based foundation level qualification which equates to IPMA (International Project Management Association) Level D.

The APMP assessment involves one three hour written essay-based paper.

APMP assesses the candidate's breadth of knowledge in all areas of project management, from strategic and commercial implications to the technical, organisational, and people management skills required to participate effectively within a project team.

Possession of the APMP qualification demonstrates knowledge of fundamental project management principles. Practitioners holding this qualification will be able to demonstrate an understanding of how these principals are applied and how they interact. In addition they will also understand how their project fits into their organisations' strategic and commercial environment.

The following documents are available from the APM website. http://www.apm.org.uk/ and should be studied along with this guide.

- APMP syllabus
- APMP Candidate Guidance Notes
- APMP sample paper

Because of the very wide diversity of sources that the APM use as reference points for the APMP syllabus it has been almost impossible for an individual to access all the necessary materials. This text has attempted to resolve that problem by distilling the required information into 1 volume.

There are two ways you can register to sit the APMP exam: by registering for a training course and exam with an Accredited Provider, or by self-study and sitting the exam on one of APM's Open events. For information on how to apply to take the APMP exam without attending a training course please contact APM Head Office; Qualifications Dept, or e-mail qualifications@apm.org.uk.

Contents

1 Projects, Programmes and Portfolios

Learning Objectives

•Define "what is a project" and "what is project management"

•Identify the differences between projects and business as usual

•Define project management processes

•Define the terms 'Programme Management' and 'Portfolio Management'

•Explain the benefits of project and programme management and the challenges faced by organisations in using them.

APMP syllabus topics 1.1, 1.2, 1.3

1.1 What is a project?

Here are three different definitions

"An endeavour in which human, material and financial resources are organised in a novel way to deliver a unique scope of work of given specification, often within constraints of cost and time, and to achieve beneficial change defined by quantitative and qualitative objectives."

The Association for Project Management

"A temporary endeavour undertaken to create a unique product, service or result."

Project Management Institute

•A unique set of coordinated activities, with definite starting and finishing points, undertaken by an individual or organisation to meet specific objectives within defined schedule, cost and performance parameters"

BS6079 (Guide to Project Management)

All of these are valid definitions from which we can determine the following key characteristics that together differentiate projects from "business as usual".

- Projects are **Unique.** When doing a project we create something that did not previously exist. Some projects are totally different whist others may contain some elements similar to previous projects. It is the unique elements of projects that make them so challenging and are the major sources of **Risk**.

- Projects are **Finite** and **Temporary**. They have a start point and an end point.

- Projects have defined **Deliverables**. Whether it is a physical product, a piece of software or a service delivery there will be a specification that defines the characteristics and quality parameters of the end product. An *Acceptance Test* will take place to determine whether the product meets the specification.

- Projects generally require **Teams** and teams need **Organising** and **Leading**

1.2 What is Project Management?

A brief description is "the controlled implementation of a defined change"
A longer description is provided by BS6079

> *'Planning, monitoring and control of all aspects of a project and the*
> *motivation of all those involved in it to achieve the project objectives*
> *on time and to the specified cost, quality and performance'*

 Planning, monitoring and controlling are the mechanical aspects of project management. The most difficult aspect of project management is the leading and motivation of the project team, especially when things are not going well. Being good at the mechanical tasks is not sufficient to make a good project manager. Leadership skills are paramount.

1.3 Project Management Processes

Project management processes are all the processes needed to execute a project from start to finish. Processes take place throughout the project life cycle and can be categorised as:-

- ➤ Initiation processes
  - o e.g Needs analysis, feasibility studies, developing product specifications, business plan development
- ➤ Planning processes
  - o e.g Activity definition, cost estimating, schedule development, resource planning
- ➤ Monitoring and controlling processes
  - o   e.g. Scope verification, quality assurance and control, change control, earned value measurement
- ➤ Closing processes
  - o e.g Administrative closeout, handover meeting, contract closure, post project review

The overall Project Management Process can be represented by the transformation diagram overleaf.

The **input** to the process is a need such as a business need or customer requirement. This need will be satisfied by the **output** of the project such as the production of specified goods or services. There will be **constraints** acting on the project such as the specification and time and cost parameters as well as external factors such as legal and environmental considerations. The project manager will have at his disposal various **mechanisms** that constitute the project resources, tools and techniques as well as the support of the owning organisation.

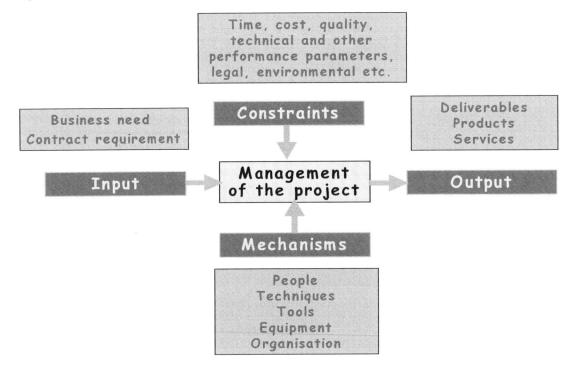

Figure 1.1 The project management process
(based on APM Body of Knowledge, 2006, P3)

1.4 Why use Project Management?

This may seem like an obvious question but it has not always been so. Project management as a defined profession with its own body of knowledge only emerged in the last third of the twentieth century. Even basic tools such as spreadsheets did not appear until the 1970s.

Nowadays organisations accept that in order to introduce change they need the disciplines inherent in formal project management. The major benefits arising from formal project management include:-

> ➢ Boundaries and constraints are determined up-front
> ➢ The tools and techniques of project management are designed to implement change efficiently.
> ➢ A business case has been made and success criteria defined
> ➢ The sponsor understands what the deliverables are and how they will be demonstrated, early in the project
> ➢ Bring order, structure and discipline to a unique and non-repeatable undertaking

- Reduce the risk of failure from poor investment decision-making, scope creep, inadequate specification, overstated benefits, under-costing etc.
- Monitoring and control processes designed to maximise the chance that deliverables are achieved
- Accountability for the project is centred on one individual, the PM
- Accountability for achieving stated benefits is also centred on one individual, the Sponsor.
- Organisations learn from Post-Project Reviews
- The project organisation is geared to change. It is multi-disciplined with few functional interests.
- Enables sharing of expensive or critical resource across projects

1.5 Projects v Operations (Business as usual)

Operations is the term used to describe the normal business processes and operations conducted by the company or organisation as it undergoes its day to day business. Much of it consists of repeatable and routine management processes. It provides the services and products for business customers on a daily and continuous basis.

It is focused on such things as:-

- Meeting business performance targets such as quality, revenue, turnover and profit targets
- Ensuring that owners, shareholder and the taxpayer get value for money
- Satisfying customer needs and requirements
- Handling issues and problems

Projects and operations have to exist side by side but have very different characteristics. Projects are **Unique** and **Finite** whereas Operations are characteristically **Repetitive** and **Ongoing.**

Projects are normally **Revolutionary** in that their outcome is normally a step change in the way something operates. Operations on the other hand are **Evolutionary** in the sense that organisations strive for continuous improvement in small non-disruptive steps.

Because of their uniqueness Projects involve **Risk and Uncertainty.** The performance of Operations is based on cumulative **Experience** that minimises or eliminates risk.
Projects are normally carried out by a **Specially Assembled Team** that only exists for the life of the project. For stability and efficiency Operations requires a **Permanent Workforce** with minimal turnover.

In summary, Projects take place in an environment that is **Dynamic and Changing** whereas the efficiency of an Operation relies on a **Stable and Predictive** environment.

1.6 Programme Management

Programme Management is the co-ordinated management of a group of projects that are inter-related and/or interdependent and contribute to a common strategic objective.

Programme Management is a strategic tool. Programmes are generally overseen by the CEO and the Board.

Projects in a programme can be in parallel or in series or a combination of both. Hence programs can be finite or ongoing

Projects within a Programme still have individual project managers who report to the programme manager who in turn reports either to a senior sponsor who could be a board member or to the board itself.

1.6.1 Benefits of Programme Management

In a complex organisation it is very easy for individual projects to lose site of overall corporate objectives. A way of avoiding this is to make sure that projects are coordinated via programme management. There are substantial benefits from this approach: e.g

- ➢ Programmes will ensure project objectives are in line with corporate objective
- ➢ There will be more efficient use of resources because they will be allocated with regard to overall programme requirements rather than individual projects
- ➢ Coordination will be carried out all across projects in the programme
- ➢ Risks are managed across the programme
- ➢ Programme Management provides a strategic tool for managing business projects and keeps the focus on the business change objectives
- ➢ Programme Management encompasses the whole Value Chain and avoids point solutions that may be sub-optimal.

1.6.2 Programme Manager Roles & Responsibilities

The principal responsibility of the programme manager is to ensure that the objectives of the programme are met. In order to do this the programme manager:-

- ➢ Must ensure that all project managers share a vision across the whole of the programme so that all project plans are fully aligned with the programme objectives

> Will act as the link between individual projects and project boards and the programme board and must ensure that all information flow both between projects and upwards to the programme board is timely and accurate.
> Must ensure that all projects are progressing in line with the requirements of the programme
> Makes sure that scarce resources are prioritised across projects for maximum programme benefit
> Acts as manager and mentor to the individual project managers

Unless asked for assistance the programme manager does not normally get involved with the detail of individual projects but is responsible for managing the interfaces between them and resolving conflicts between them.

1.7 Portfolio Management

There are two overlapping definitions of what we mean by a portfolio.

a)   In a total business context a portfolio is defined as the totality of all an organisation's programmes, projects and related operational activities.

b)   A portfolio can also be described as a set of projects or programmes that have no interdependencies and do not share a common objective. Projects may share resources but they are otherwise unconnected. Portfolio management is particularly concerned with the management of resources across competing projects and programmes with particular regard to:-

> Scarce or limited resources and capacity bottlenecks
> Balance across the portfolio between risk and return
> Timing of the project i.e. when it takes place

Portfolio managers must ensure that senior management are provided with all the information they require in order to make appropriate decisions regarding the portfolio and will assist and influence them in making those decisions and making sure that the portfolio supports the strategy of the organisation. This is an aspect of Corporate Governance (Chapter 4).

1.7.1   Benefits of managing groups of projects as a portfolio

> There is a strategic link between programmes, projects and BAU operations to ensure that all the activities of the organisation are supporting business objectives.

➢ The same governance principles are applied to all organisational activities. (see chapter 4)

➢ Resource allocation considers the requirements of the entire organisation so that an optimum balance can be made between projects and BAU

➢ Risks and returns can be optimised across the entire portfolio

➢ There will be a more efficient integration of the output of projects into operations

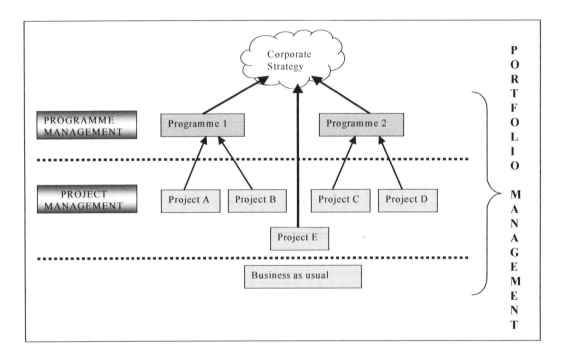

Figure 1.2 Relationship between project, programme and portfolio management
(based on APM Body of Knowledge, 2006, P7)

1.8 Key Differences Between Programmes and Portfolios

➢ Projects in a Programme are always inter-related and interdependent whereas projects in a Portfolio can have no dependencies apart from possible resource conflicts.

➢ Projects in a Programme all contribute to the same defined strategic objective. A portfolio can support several strategic objectives.

➢ In a Programme all projects must usually succeed for the programme to succeed whereas in a Portfolio failures can be compensated by successes in other projects.

➢ As all elements of a programme contribute to the same strategic goals the programme manager can switch resources and priorities between projects. This is less true with portfolios.

1.9 Challenges

In order to maintain competitiveness and to comply with corporate governance requirements, organisations must become proficient at managing projects and programmes. It takes a lot of planning and effort to make this happen and organisations face many challenges in creating an efficient project environment.

They must be prepared to:-

- ➢ Recruit and reward experienced project managers
- ➢ Invest in training of project personnel
- ➢ Empower project/programme managers to make decisions within defined limits
- ➢ Change to a more appropriate organisational structure e.g from weak matrix to strong matrix (Chapter 3)
- ➢ Implement standard methods and procedures
- ➢ Put in place project/programme sponsorship and steering committees/boards with appropriate management training
- ➢ Continuously seek to improve performance

In developing project management capability, organisations progress through different levels of competency. This is illustrated in the Project Management Maturity Model below.

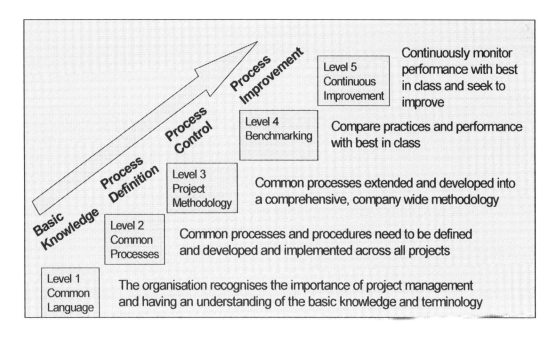

Figure 1.3 Project Management Maturity Model (Harold Kerzner)

2 Project Context

Learning Objectives

•Understand what is meant by Project Context

•Understand how to carry out an Environmental Impact Analysis (EIA) using tools such as PESTLE & SWOT

APMP syllabus topic 1.4

2.1 Definition

Projects do not take place in a vacuum. They take place within a "context" or "environment" and the successful accomplishment of a project generally requires a significant sensitivity to, and appreciation of, the context in which it is based.

Some of these environmental factors are within the control of the project personnel but many are not. Many of them can significantly affect the project outcome hence they need to be monitored. Generic examples of the kind of things that make up the project context are shown in fig 2.1 below. These include elements that cover both the internal and external environment of the projects. The project/programme manager and the project sponsor share a responsibility for monitoring the project context. In general terms the project manager would be primarily concerned with the internal environment and the sponsor with the external environment.

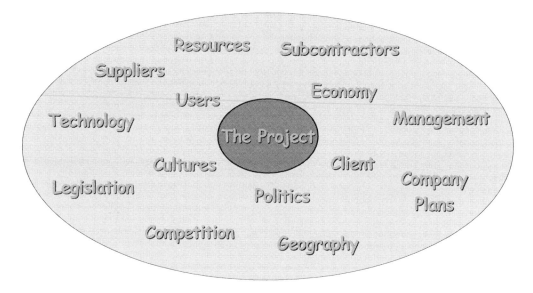

Figure 2.1 Project Context Examples

Note that the word environment is not used here in the "green" sense and project context would exclude elements totally under the control of the PM such as team management issues.

2.2 Environmental Impact Analysis (EVA)

An EVA should be carried out as early in the project as possible, typically during the Feasibility stage. The elements identified as being significant will then be continuously monitored. It effectively constitutes part of Risk Management planning (Chapter13). There are two principal tools that can be used to facilitate an EVA. They are PESTLE and SWOT.

2.2.1 PESTLE Analysis

PESTLE is an acronym that stands for:-

Political
Economic
Sociological
Technological
Legal / Regulatory
Ethical/Environmental

It is simply a tool for providing some structure to the analysis. Possible examples under each of the headings are as follows:-

- Political
  - Taxation
  - Government Policies
- Economic
  - Interest rates
  - Economic outlook
- Social
  - Current Fashions
  - Demographics

- Technology
  - eCommerce
  - Leading edge
- Legal
  - Employment law
  - Environmental regulations
- Ethical
  - Job losses
  - 3rd world exploitation

2.2.2 SWOT Analysis

SWOT stands for Strengths, Weaknesses, Opportunities and Threats. It is another useful tool for studying both the internal and external environments of projects or of organisations. Strengths and weaknesses will generally be found more within the internal environment. Examples are product and project portfolios, production facilities, staff, IT systems etc. Opportunities and threats generally arise from the external environment. It can be seen that the PESTLE elements above are biased towards external factors.

Both PESTLE and SWOT analyses are best carried out by "Brainstorming" using members of the project team and appropriate stakeholders.

SWOT analysis can be carried out at any level of detail ranging from a whole organisation to a sub-project or product.

3 Project Organisation

Learning Objectives

• Understand the role of the Project Sponsor and the importance of project sponsorship

• Describe the role of the project board

• Describe the different roles and responsibilities within a project team

• Describe functional, matrix and projectised team organisational models and their advantages and disadvantages

• Describe the functions and benefits of a Project Office

3.1 Project Organisation Structure

The figure below shows a typical project structure.

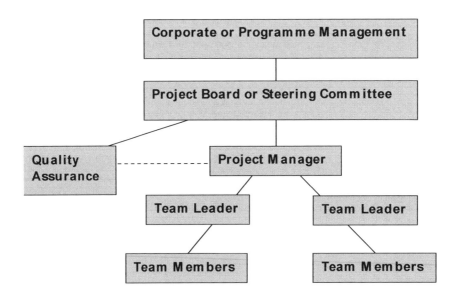

Figure 3.1 Project Organisation Structure

The above structure is based on Prince 2 but similar structures are widely used.

3.2 The Project Board

The project board oversees the project from initiation to benefits realisation under the chairmanship of the Project Sponsor. The PM will formally report to the Board at regular intervals and at "Gate" reviews (paragraph 5.4.1)

A typical make up of a Board is as follows:-

- ➤ Project Sponsor (Chair)
- ➤ Client (if appropriate)
- ➤ End user representative
- ➤ Key Suppliers/Sub-contractors
- ➤ Appropriate functional managers
- ➤ The Project Sponsor

3.2.1 The Project Sponsor

It is vital that a project has an effective sponsor. The sponsor carries overall responsibility for the project from feasibility to benefits realisation. For a successful project there needs to be a continuing dialogue between sponsor and project manager.

The sponsor needs to be:-

  ➢ A manager with enough seniority to work across organisational boundaries
  ➢ Be an effective Champion of the project and the change it will bring about
  ➢ Have enough knowledge of project management to judge the effectiveness of the project
  ➢ Be supportive of the project manager and have sufficient time to allocate to the role

The role of the sponsor is likely to be more effective in a mature organisation.

3.2.2 Sponsor responsibilities

  ➢ Chair the Project Board
  ➢ Make the business case
  ➢ Be the project Champion
  ➢ Obtain approval for expenditure
  ➢ Make sure business benefits are realised
  ➢ Terminate the project if necessary
  ➢ Determine the relative priority of Time, Cost & Quality (See 3.2.4)

3.2.3 Sponsor activities

  ➢ Define the project's success criteria
  ➢ Define the business investment aims
  ➢ Initiate the project and ensure a project manager is appointed
  ➢ Support the project manager
  ➢ Monitor project progress & make control decisions when necessary
  ➢ Monitor the project's external environment/context
  ➢ Keep senior management informed

3.2.4 The Project Management Triangle

The interaction of Time, Cost and Quality/Performance is usually represented by the Project Management Triangle depicted overleaf. It is also sometimes referred to as the triple constraint. In the centre of the triangle lies Health & Safety and Customer Satisfaction. These should be paramount on any project

It is rare that a project goes exactly to plan. There will be changes, both planned and unplanned and the whole project is subject to risk and uncertainty. When deviations occur one or more of the triple constraints has to give. For example if a project is behind schedule more resources may be needed to catch up. This will increase cost. If the budget is fixed then it may be necessary to reduce quality or functionality. The responsibility for making such decisions lies with the Sponsor and his Board. The job of the project manager is to advise on the possible options and their implications.

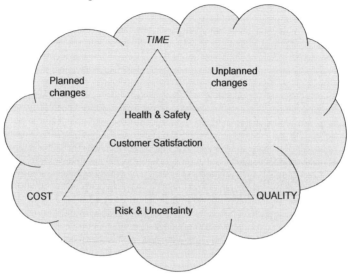

Figure 3.2 The Project Management Triangle

Projects take place in a cloud of uncertainty. The Project Manager is constantly maintaining a balance between time, cost and quality with due regard to health and safety and with the constant goal of achieving customer satisfaction.

3.3 The Project Manager

The job of the Project Manager can be summed up with 4 key roles and 6 major activities.

3.3.1 The 4 Key Project Management Roles

➢ **Integrator**:
  o Project Integration involves all those activities needed to ensure that people, procedures and work of the project is carried out in a coordinated fashion. The project manager is the only person aware of all the project activities and how they relate to each other.

- ➤ **Communicator:**
  - o The project manager must ensure that efficient communication channels are set up within the project organisation. A project manager who fails to disseminate information on time can become the major bottleneck in a project.
- ➤ **Leader:**
  - o Leadership is not the same as management. The project manager must be able to solve problems, guide people from different areas, co-ordinate the project and lead by example.
- ➤ **Decision Maker:**
  - o The project manager must have the self confidence to make key decisions even if some risk is involved. A key aspect of project management is knowing when to make a decision and when to consult the sponsor.

3.3.2 The 6 Major Project Management Activities
- ➤ **Planning:**
  - o Making sure plans are in place to meet the project objectives
- ➤ **Organising/Integrating:**
  - o Co-ordination of the mixture of human, financial and physical assets
- ➤ **Monitoring**
  - o Monitoring progress in relation to time, cost & quality and customer satisfaction
- ➤ **Controlling**
  - o Taking corrective action when actual performance deviates from the plan
- ➤ **Leading/Motivating**
  - o Leading and motivating the team and seeing to the needs of individuals
- ➤ **Reporting/Communicating**
  - o Keeping stakeholders informed of progress and issues

3.4 The Project Team & Team Leaders

On all but the smallest projects there will generally be a team leader or leaders to whom the project manager will delegate the necessary authority to execute agreed work packages. The project manager manages the project team members through the team leaders. The team leaders themselves will obviously require project management skills.

It is important that all the team members are aware of, and are committed to the overall project goals so that they can work together towards a common goal and hopefully a shared reward. This aspect will be explored further in chapters 19 and 20.

3.5 The End Users

The end users are defined as the group of people who are intended to benefit from the project. It is important to realise that they are your ultimate customers and they will be the arbiters of the quality of your deliverables. It is possible to deliver a project on time, to budget and to the specification. However if the end users are not satisfied then the project has failed. To guard against this it is of crucial importance that end user representatives are closely involved in specifying the requirements and in devising acceptance tests for the deliverables. They should be consulted and kept informed throughout the project life cycle.

3.6 Quality Assurance

The Quality Assurance function reports directly to the project board. It is concerned with the correct governance of the project (Chapter 4). It has no powers to interfere in the management of the project but will carry out regular Quality Assurance reviews and inform the board as to the outcome.

3.7 Project Team Structures

There are three basic types of project team structure:-

1. Functional
2. Projectised
3. Matrix Structures
    o   Weak
    o   Balanced
    o   Strong

3.7.1 Functional Structure

Used mainly where the project lies entirely or mainly within a single Function, or where a project passes from Function to Function e.g. product development. Often used for less important projects or in organisations with no project management culture. An example structure is shown below.

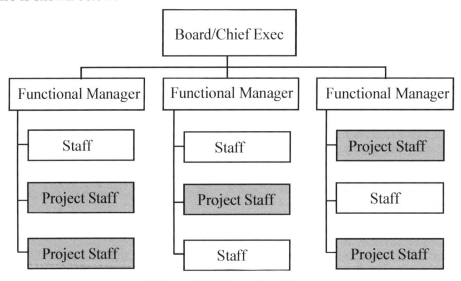

Figure 3.3 Functional structure

There may or may not be a named project manager/leader/coordinator within particular functions or covering the whole project. However such a person will have minimal power within their function and virtually none outside it. *The Functional Managers coordinate all the activities and make all the major decisions.*

3.7.2 Projectised Structure

Projectised structures represent the other extreme from Functional Structures. Such project structures are typically used by organisations whose main business consists of large capital projects such as roads, bridges, tunnels and large buildings. In this situation the project manager has total control over all resources and reports directly to a senior executive.

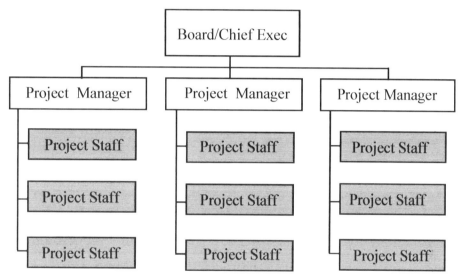

Fig 3.4 Projectised Structure.

3.8 Comparing Functional and Projectised Structures

3.8.1 Functional Structure

Positive factors
- Good technical communication
- Project linked to career development
- Development of centres of excellence
- Concentration on the business of the function
- Flexible resourcing

Negative factors
- Long communication between functions
- Functional priorities can override project

- ➢ No external customer to focus on
- ➢ Project manager has little authority
- ➢ Hinders development of non-specialised Project Managers

3.8.2 Projectised Structure

Positive Factors
- ➢ Short project communications
- ➢ Project manager has total authority and accountability
- ➢ Customer focus
- ➢ Resource dedicated to the project
- ➢ Aids PM development
- ➢ No Functional loyalties

Negative Factors
- ➢ Loss of centres of excellence
- ➢ Can be difficult to terminate
- ➢ Career progression for team members may be unclear
- ➢ Different projects teams may develop different ways of working

3.9 Weak Matrix Structure

A weak matrix structure is very similar to a functional structure except that some responsibility for coordination has been delegated to project staff. There is usually a named project manager/leader/coordinator but with limited authority, especially outside their own function.

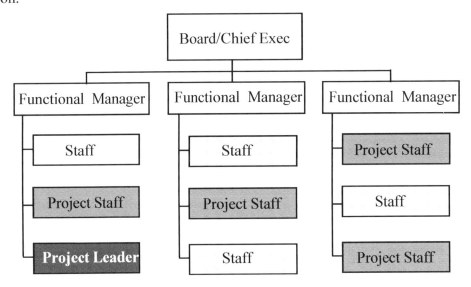

Figure 3.5 Weak Matrix Structure

3.10 Balanced Matrix Structure

In a balanced matrix there is a named project manager with referent power from the functional manager and from the CEO. The project manager coordinates all project activities. Power is balanced between project and functional managers. The structure appears identical to a weak matrix.

3.11 Strong Matrix Structure

A strong matrix is a radical change from weak and balanced matrices. Project managers now operate from a separate function under their own management which reports directly to the CEO. The PM is now fully independent of the functional managers and once functional managers allocate staff to a project they are under the control of the project manager. As in the other matrix structures, the functional managers retain line management responsibility for their staff but their day to day project activities are controlled by the PM or his/her delegates.

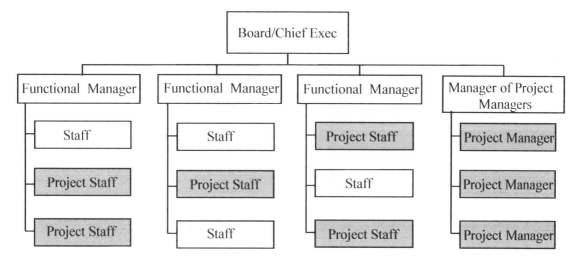

Figure 3.6 Strong Matrix Structure

The way that the relative powers of the project and functional managers varies across the organisational types is illustrated by the figure opposite.

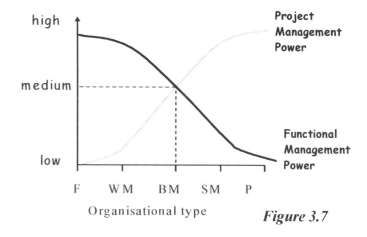

Figure 3.7

3.12 Advantages of Managing in a Matrix Organisation

- ➢ **Expertise**
  - o The skills and expertise of all the Functions are available to the project

- ➢ **Commonality**
  - o Because the project is cross functional it will tend to adopt company wide policies, procedures and methodologies which will give consistency of approach

- ➢ **Resource utilisation**
  - o In a matrix organisation it is easier to share resources between different projects leading to more efficient use of resource

- ➢ **Line management**
  - o Because team members still have functional managers the PM does not have this added workload. Also, he/she does not have to worry about their deployment after project completion.

- ➢ **PM power**
  - o The PM usually has considerably more power than in a Functional structure

- ➢ **Sub-optimisation**
  - o Avoids point solutions tended to by Functional approaches

3.13 Disadvantages of Managing in a Matrix Organisation

- ➢ **Functional conflicts**
  - o There may be conflict between the different functions, especially if things go wrong

- ➢ **Functional loyalties**
  - o Team members may feel more loyalty to their function than to the project

- ➢ **Conflict between projects**
  - o In a multi project environment a PM will fight for his project even if this is not optimal for the company

- ➢ **Lack of ownership**
  - o In a matrix environment some functions may not fully support the project especially when most of the benefits occur elsewhere

- ➢ **Communications**
    - o Communications in a matrix organisation are always more complex than in functional or projectised

- ➢ **PM power**
    - o Compared to projectised organisations PM has less power.

3.14 Factors Affecting Choice of Organisation

- ➢ **Size & complexity of the project**
    - o Increasing complexity favours a move away from Functional towards Matrix or Projectised

- ➢ **Organisational culture**
    - o Some company cultures restrict all projects to Functional or Weak matrix

- ➢ **Business scope of the project**
    - o Multi-Function projects, especially if complex are unlikely to be managed Functionally

- ➢ **Business criticality**
    - o Projects which are business critical require at least a balanced matrix structure

- ➢ **Where in the organisation the benefits accrue**
    - o If benefits accrue mainly to a single function then it makes sense for that function to manage the project

- ➢ **Skills & resources available**
    - o Similarly if most of the required resources lie within a function.

Be aware that some projects may exhibit different structures in different phases. For instance the Design phase could be within a single function then a matrix organisation could be used for Implementation.

4 Project Governance & Methodology

Learning Objectives

• Describe the typical contents of a structured method (methodology) and the advantages of adopting such methods

•Describe the principles of governance of project management

•Describe the functions and benefits of a Project Office

APMP syllabus topic 1.6, 8.9, 8.10

4.1 Project Methodologies

A Project Methodology is a collection of Policies, Procedures, Guidelines, Templates and Methods which together define how projects should be run in an organisation. Methodologies can be either Public or Proprietary. The best know public methodology is Prince 2 (**Pr**ojects **in** **C**ontrolled **E**nvironment) which amongst Government departments, local government, utility companies and British based companies has become the UK's de facto standard for managing projects. However, large multinational corporations such as IBM and HP tend to develop their own proprietary methodologies appropriate to their needs.

Without standard methods project management is practiced in an ad-hoc and inconsistent manner. Project managers develop their own ways of working and reporting. This leads to inefficiencies such as "constant reinvention of the wheel" and makes it harder for staff to move between projects. Combining project results for upward reporting becomes a difficult task. For organisations that do not have a methodology a good starting point is to develop some standard documents and procedures and then build on the experience.

4.1.1 Typical components of a Methodology

The contents of a methodology can vary tremendously depending on the complexity of the organisation and the complexity of the projects they carry out. However all methodologies should cover the following basic requirements.

- ➢ Suggested projects organisational structures
- ➢ Defined roles, responsibilities and authority levels
- ➢ Defined life cycle or cycles
- ➢ Mandatory policies and procedures for project initiation, execution, phase reviews and project closure etc
- ➢ Inputs and outputs for each life cycle phase
- ➢ Reporting standards
- ➢ Methods, Processes and tools for carrying out project activities e.g Risk Management, Change Control, Quality Assurance, Earned Value, Procurement etc
- ➢ Document templates e.g. Project Management Plan, Functional Specification, Quality Plan, Risk Plan etc
- ➢ Lessons learned archives

4.1.2 Benefits of using a Methodology

- ➢ Provides a clear and consistent approach with agreed decision points along the way
- ➢ Standardisation of methods and processes across all projects
- ➢ Faster implementation time as less effort is spent reinventing the wheel each time
- ➢ Common formats allow for roll-up of projects for a corporate viewpoint
- ➢ Encourages learning from project to project through a structured approach
- ➢ Fewer misunderstandings through using a common language
- ➢ A common format makes project handover easier

- ➢ Fewer conflicts as clear roles and responsibilities are defined up front
- ➢ Effective communication between the various parties involved in the project
- ➢ Checklists and standard approach reduces support needs for less experienced project managers.
- ➢ Shows commitment from senior management to the implementation of projects
- ➢ Facilitates better project governance and continuous improvement in project management processes

4.2 Corporate Governance

Corporate governance is the system by which companies are directed and controlled for the benefit of shareholders.

It provides:-

- ➢ The structure through which organisational goals are set
- ➢ The means by which the goals are to be met
- ➢ The monitoring of performance against those goals

Boards of directors are responsible for the governance of their companies.

Figure 4.1
(APM Body of Knowledge. 2006. P98)

4.3 Project Governance

Project Governance is a subset of Corporate Governance and concerns those areas specifically related to project activities.

As is shown in figure 4.1, most of the day to day management of projects lies outside the domain of Corporate Governance.

Effective Project Governance ensures:-

- ➢ The Project portfolio is aligned to Corporate goals and strategies
- ➢ Projects are financially and technically justified
- ➢ Projects are controlled at a high level via ongoing reviews
- ➢ The Board and major stakeholders are provided with timely, relevant and accurate information
- ➢ There will be fewer project failures
- ➢ The interests of directors, project staff, stockholders and other stakeholders are aligned

> Less surprises and more predictable performance

4.3.1 Failures of Project Governance

Projects fail for many reasons but a common cause is lack of engagement by the Board with ongoing projects. This failure of engagement can present itself in many ways as in the following examples.

> No clear link between project deliverables and Corporate goals
> No agreed measures of success
> Lack of effective senior management Sponsorship
> Poor engagement with Senior Stakeholders
> Lack of application of project methodologies
> Poor or no risk management
> Lack of contact with Suppliers at senior levels
> Project acquisition driven by price rather than long term value
> Too little attention to breaking down projects into manageable steps

4.3.2 The 4 key components of Governance

1. Portfolio Direction

All projects within the Portfolio should be aligned with Corporate goals and objectives. An acid test for the relevance of a project is to ask in what way is it contributing to the goals of the organisation.

2. Project Sponsorship

All projects should have an appropriate Sponsor to whom the PM reports and who owns the budget and the business case. Without such a sponsor the link to Corporate goals is lost and projects can be allowed to go out of control.

3. Project Management Effectiveness

Project teams should have the skills and competence to achieve project objectives and be given appropriate tools and resources. There should be effective delegation.

4. Disclosure and Reporting

Project reports will provide timely and accurate information that supports the organisations decision making process. There should be a culture of open and honest disclosure and lack of fear of being the bearer of bad news.

4.4 Governance Principles

> Projects should be clearly linked to key business objectives
> There should be clear senior management ownership of project
> There should be effective engagement with stakeholders

- ➤ Leaders must have the required project and risk management skills
- ➤ There should be appropriate contact at senior level with key suppliers
- ➤ Projects should be driven by long term value rather than short term cost
- ➤ Projects should be broken down into manageable steps

4.5 The Project Office

All organisations that take project management seriously will have a project office that exists to support the organisation's project needs. Major projects and/or programmes may have their own dedicated support office. Where a project office does not exist the services must be provided from within the project.

At its simplest level the project office may just provide administrative support to project personnel. At the other extreme can become the "Centre of Excellence" for project management and the body to which project managers report. It will be the overseeing body for all project activity and be responsible for linking corporate strategy to project execution.

The Project Office can have various names depending on the organisation and the extent of its role e.g.

- ➤ PSO -Project Support Office

- ➤ PPSO-Projects and Programmes Support Office

- ➤ PMO-Project Management Office

- ➤ EPMO-Enterprise Programme Management Office

4.5.1 Project Office Functions and Benefits

As a basic minimum a project office should provide the following functions:-

- ➤ Administrative support to project managers and team members
- ➤ Consolidation of individual project status reports into programme and corporate reports including exception reporting
- ➤ Project process quality audit and assurance

Other possible functions are:-

- ➤ Identification and development of PM methodology, standards, documents, templates etc
- ➤ Co-ordination of resource allocation across all projects
- ➤ Selection, operation and management of project tools such as enterprise wide project management software

- ➢ Consolidation and dissemination of lessons learned
- ➢ Development and management of PM job descriptions and training programmes and professional development.
- ➢ Organisation of mentoring and skills development
- ➢ Coordination of risk management initiatives across projects and programmes
- ➢ Ensuring that individual project goals remain consistent with programme and corporate goals

The presence of a project office allows an organisation to draw together its project management expertise, and makes possible the development of that expertise into a centre of excellence. A project management office fits particularly well with a strong matrix organisation as project managers and project office staff can be brought under common management. However for functional and weak/balanced structures some sort of project office is vital in order to facilitate a common approach to managing projects.

5 Project Life Cycles and Reviews

Learning Objectives

• Describe the phases of a project that make up the project life cycle

• Understand the need for phasing in projects

• Understand the meaning of extended life cycle

• Describe the various kinds of project reviews

APMP syllabus topics 6.1, 6.6

5.1 A Generic Lifecycle

A project life cycle consists of a sequence of distinct phases or stages. There are many varieties of life cycles which vary across different industries and organisations. Shown below is a generic lifecycle which can be applied to many different kinds of project.

Figure 5.1 A Generic Lifecycle

In the **Concept** phase the need/problem/opportunity emerges and the proposed solution is tested for technical and financial feasibility. At this stage plans may be at a very low level of details and estimates of costs and timescales are at a low level of accuracy. Plans only need to be accurate enough to decide whether the project is worth continuing into the next phase.

The **Definition** phase is where detailed plans are formulated and if the project is still feasible it will progress to the **Implementation** stage. This stage is often broken down into further sub-phases. Upon completion and acceptance by the client the **Handover** takes place and the **Closeout** phase formally **closes** the project down.

5.2 The Extended Project Life Cycle

In the Extended Project Life Cycle illustrated below, the Operational and Termination phases of the project deliverables are included. This is the life cycle referred to in BS6079 – The British Standard guide to project management. However most authorities refer to this as a **Product** life cycle as projects are considered complete once **Handover** takes place

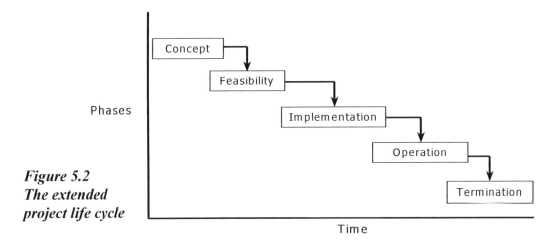

*Figure 5.2
The extended
project life cycle*

Note that there are no universally accepted names for project phases. **Concept** often includes **Feasibility** and vice versa and the first phase is sometimes called **Initiation.**

Design & Development are sometimes treated as separate phases or often just referred to as the **Planning** phase or the **Definition** phase.

The **Implementation** phase is often called the **Execution** phase.

Closeout is often referred to as the **Exit** phase.

5.3 Benefits of Phasing

The following are some of the benefits that arise from breaking project into phases.

> ➢ Identification smaller chunks of work that are more manageable in terms of time, cost and specification
> ➢ Provide sponsor/manager checkpoints and gate review points
> ➢ Encourage rolling-wave planning*
> ➢ Improves the accuracy of estimating
> ➢ Focuses on the right work at the right time in the right order
> ➢ Application of specialist resource to each phase
> ➢ Reduce the risk by committing to a phase at a time
> ➢ Phase completion shows evidence of progress

*Rolling-wave planning is where activities taking place in the near future are planned in depth whilst those further out, in later phases, are planned in outline only. Thus as time passes the planning "wave" advances.

5.4 Project Reviews

There are several types of project reviews and there is no consistency in vocabulary between organisations and this can cause confusion.

5.4.1 Phase, Stage or Gate reviews

This review is carried out at the end of each project Phase/Stage*.The boundaries between Phases/Stages are sometimes known as "gateways". At each gateway the project manager must report back to the project board or sponsor and ask for authority to "pass through the gate" i.e. proceed to the next phase. The board will review progress to date against the original baseline plan and any approved changes. They should also revisit the business case

*Where a phase has major components it may be broken down into sub-phases or stages.

in order to determine if it is still valid. The main benefits of this process are that bad projects can be stopped before too much money has been spent whilst good projects will increase management confidence and commitment.

5.4.2 Project Status reviews

Project Evaluation reviews can be carried out either routinely at set intervals are as a result of a trigger e.g.

➢ Major milestone reached
➢ Project crisis
➢ Major scope changes
➢ Change of management

The review could cover the whole project or just particular aspects. e.g.

➢ Technical issues
➢ Resources
➢ Governance
➢ Schedule and budget
➢ Requirements
➢ Business case

5.4.3 Project Audits

These reviews typically are concerned with Governance and are covered in Chapter 14 (Quality)

5.4.4 Post Project Review/Lessons Learned Review

This is a review of the management of the project and is carried out at the end of the project. Prince 2 calls this the Project Evaluation Review. It is covered under Chapter 22 (Handover & Closure)

5.4.5 Benefits Realisation review/Post Implementation review

This is an evaluation of the project outcome compared to that predicted in the Business Plan. It is covered in Chapter 8 (Requirements, Benefits Management & Success Criteria). Prince 2 confusingly calls this the Post Project Review.

6 The Business Case

Learning Objectives

•Explain the purpose and contents of a Business Case

•Describe the authorship and ownership of the Business Case

•Explain investment appraisal techniques

  –Payback
  –Internal rate of return
  –Net present value

APMP syllabus topic 5.1

6.1 Building the Business Case

6.1.1 Business Case Objective & Purpose

The objective in developing a Business Case is to provide a justification for carrying out the project. It must show the expected costs and benefits of the project and how it fits in with the company strategy and contributes to the corporate goals of the organisation. Not all costs and benefits are tangible, i.e. they cannot easily be expressed in purely monetary terms.

In any organisation there are usually many proposed projects that are competing for limited funds. Therefore the purpose of the Business Case is not just to demonstrate why a project is viable in its own right but also why it should be favoured over others.

The Business Case is prepared very early in the project life cycle. As normally no detailed planning has taken place it is often difficult to decide the level of detail in the Business Plan. The answer is that it should contain enough information to enable a decision to be made as to whether to carry on with the project. The decision can always be modified in the light of more detailed planning.

Every project must in some way contribute to the corporate goals of the organisation.

6.1.2 Contents of a Business Case

- Description of Problem/Opportunity and Scope outline
- Other options (including do nothing)
- Principal reason for carrying it out
- Project Deliverables/Objectives
- Fit to the organisation's business strategy
- Emphasis on Time/Cost/Quality
- Outline Schedule and Major Milestones
- Investments Appraisal
- Expected Costs & Benefits-Both tangible and intangible
- High Level Risks and Assumptions
- Success Criteria
- Assumptions
- Stakeholder Analysis
- Impact on Business as Usual

6.1.3 Constructing a Business Case

In order to construct a business case it is necessary to estimate the costs and expected benefits of the project and produce a budget and schedule. This is effectively the first attempt at a project plan and it is carried out by performing the steps shown in fig 6.1 below. It is an iterative process which will become more accurate as the project progresses, experience is gained and more knowledge is obtained.

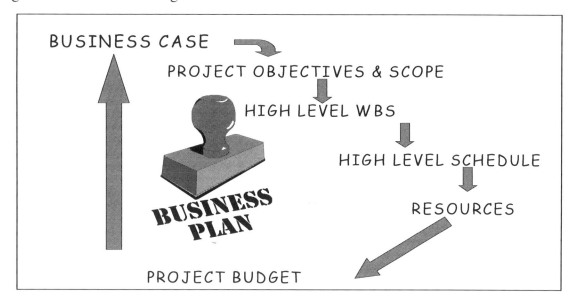

Figure 6.1 Business Plan Construction

The Business Case will make clear the balance between the expected costs and benefits of the project and the level of risk involved. As the project develops and the true costs and risks emerge it should be continuously reviewed to check that the project continues to meet the business objectives. If not there may be a case for termination or scope change.

6.1.4 Key Contributors to the Business Case

The Sponsor
The Sponsor owns the Business Case and has overall responsibility to the CEO for its production and realisation. This responsibility extends beyond project completion and into operation.

The Project Manager
Ideally the project manager should work with the Sponsor to produce the Business Case and agree the outline budget and schedule and Key Performance Indicators. However in many cases the PM is not appointed at this stage. In that situation the PM should study the business case and discuss any issues with the Sponsor. The PM will also make sure that the project team is aware of the main points of the business case.

Technical Analyst/Consultant
There needs to be an appropriately skilled person who can verify the technical feasibility of the project.

Financial Accountant
Similarly there needs to be someone to verify the financial feasibility.

Client/End user
Where appropriate an end user representative should confirm the objectives and requirements.

6.2 Investment Appraisal

6.2.1 Payback
Payback is the simplest of all the project evaluation tools but produces the least meaningful results. All this method does is to calculate how long it takes for cash flow to break even; i.e. when costs equal benefits.

This method ignores cash flows after break-even point and ignores the changing value of money over time. It should only be used in conjunction with other methods such as IRR.

6.2.2 Discounted Cash Flow & Net Present Value
When trying to ascertain the value of a project we start with the cash flow forecast. However if we simply add up all the costs and benefits over time we ignore the fact that payment today is worth more than the same payment in the future. This is because inflation erodes the value of money. It is also difficult to compare two or more different cash flows to see which gives most value. The Net Present Value (NPV) method uses Discounted Cash Flow (DCF) to convert any cash flow to a single value. The first step is to calculate the Present value (PV) for every element of the cash flow.

For a given future payment **t** years from now $\quad PV = M_t / (1 + r)^t$

M_t = amount of payment **t** years from now
r - interest rate (sometimes called "discount rate")   **t** - time period(year)

Thus the Present Value of £1 in 2 years time at a discount rate of 10%

$$= 1/(1.1)^2 \quad = 0.8264$$

Such values can be worked out for every year/discount rate combination or they can be obtained from the table below. Totalling the PV for every year gives us the NPV for the project cash flow. This value can then be used to judge the project viability, both stand alone and in comparison with other projects.

Discount Rate

Years		1%	2%	3%	4%	5%	6%	7%	8%	9%	10%
	0	1.000	1.000	1.000	1.000	1.000	1.000	1.000	1.000	1.000	1.000
	1	0.990	0.980	0.971	0.962	0.952	0.943	0.935	0.926	0.917	0.909
	2	0.980	0.961	0.943	0.925	0.907	0.890	0.873	0.857	0.842	0.826
	3	0.971	0.942	0.915	0.889	0.864	0.840	0.816	0.794	0.772	0.751
	4	0.961	0.924	0.888	0.855	0.823	0.792	0.763	0.735	0.708	0.683
	5	0.951	0.906	0.863	0.822	0.784	0.747	0.713	0.681	0.650	0.621
	6	0.942	0.888	0.837	0.790	0.746	0.705	0.666	0.630	0.596	0.564
	7	0.933	0.871	0.813	0.760	0.711	0.665	0.623	0.583	0.547	0.513
	8	0.923	0.853	0.789	0.731	0.677	0.627	0.582	0.540	0.502	0.467
	9	0.914	0.837	0.766	0.703	0.645	0.592	0.544	0.500	0.460	0.424
	10	0.905	0.820	0.744	0.676	0.614	0.558	0.508	0.463	0.422	0.386

Figure 6.2 Discount Rates

The example below illustrates how we can use the values from the table above to calculate the NPV for any cash flow. For this example we have used a discount rate of 10%.

Cash Flow	Year	Discount Factor	Present Value
-100	0	1.000	-£100.00
20	1	0.909	£18.18
60	2	0.826	£49.56
40	3	0.751	£30.04
40	4	0.683	£27.32
30	5	0.621	£18.63
£90	Net Present Value		£43.73

Thus it can be seen that an overall project profit of £90K is reduced to about £44k when we assume that the cash flow is discounted at 10%/annum. If we were choosing between projects purely based on profit we would choose the one with the highest NPV. If we can borrow money at 10% then the project will generate a profit of £44K at today's values

6.2.3 Selecting the Discount Rate

In the above example we have used a discount rate of 10%. Different rates will give different answers so in real life how is a discount rate selected? There are 4 main factors affecting discount rates:-

> Interest rates
> Inflation rates
> Perceived risks to the project
> Opportunity costs (the opportunity we forgo by investing in this project)

The current and forecast values of these parameters will be used to determine the discount rate to be used. Discount rates are normally set at Corporate level and reviewed regularly. Typically there will be a range of values depending on the perceived risk to the project, higher risks requiring higher discount rates.

Definition of Net Present Value:
The value today of a future cash flow stream discounted using a particular discount rate.

6.2.4 Internal Rate of Return (IRR)

The difficulties of selecting an appropriate discount rate can be overcome if we turn the problem around. Instead of selecting a rate and then seeing if the project is profitable at that rate we can work out what the rate would have to be make the costs and benefits of the project equal each other. In other words what rate would produce a NPV of zero. This could be calculated using a spreadsheet function or done manually by iteration.

For example in the previous example a rate of 10% produces a NPV of £43.73K. If we repeat the exercise using a discount rate of 20% we will find that the NPV falls to £12.4k. Increasing the rate to 30% causes the return to fall below zero to -£8.7k. If we interpolate between these two values we can determine that the rate at which the NPV is zero is about 26%. Thus for that particular project the IRR is about 26%.

Definition of Internal Rate of Return:
The discount rate which makes the present value of costs equal to the present value of benefits thus giving a NPV of zero.

6.2.5 Limitations of Investment Appraisal Techniques

Although it is important to understand the financial implications of a project the techniques do have their limitations.

> **Accuracy of estimates**

Investment Appraisal involves forecasting the future. This could involve forecasting sales revenues, efficiency savings, productivity improvements etc. These values are arrived at by the expertise and judgement of the people involved but they are just estimates and they will invariably be wrong.

> ### Bias and unrealistic expectations

On any project there will be those in favour and those against. Those in favour will tend to stress the benefits and try and minimise the potential costs and those against will do the reverse. Many projects are approved based on unrealistic expectations.

> ### Strategic Considerations

It is often necessary to take on projects which are not profitable, for strategic reasons. It may be necessary to defend a market position or to open new markets or to improve prospects of future business.

> ### Legislation

New rules and regulations are constantly being imposed on organisations. They usually involve health and safety or environmental considerations. They have to be obeyed regardless of cost unless the organisation withdraws from the affected operations.

> ### Intangible costs

Not all costs or benefits can be expressed in terms of money. Many beneficial projects can not be justified on cash terms. The main benefits can arise in improving quality of life, for example building a hospital or a bypass.

6.2.6 Comparison of Methods

Payback Period

> ### Advantages
>   - Very simple to apply
>   - Easy to understand and communicate

> ### Disadvantages
>   - Ignores cash flow beyond payback
>   - Ignores discounting effect of time
>   - Cash flow estimate may not be accurate

NPV/IRR

- ➢ **Advantages**
    - ○ Takes account of all future cash flow
    - ○ Takes account of time value of money

- ➢ **Disadvantages**
    - ○ More difficult to calculate
    - ○ NPV is highly dependant on discount factor
    - ○ Cash flow estimate may not be accurate
    - ○ NPV not good for comparing projects of unequal size.

7 Managing Stakeholders

Learning Objectives

•Describe a Stakeholder Management process

•Explain the importance of Stakeholder Management

APMP syllabus topic 2.2

7.1 The Importance of Stakeholder Management

A Stakeholder is defined as any person or body that has an interest in a project or its outcome or is affected by it. Stakeholder Management involves the processes of identifying stakeholders, analysing their interest and formulating plans to control or influence them.

The attitude and actions of Stakeholders can have a significant effect on the performance and outcome of your project and hence they must be proactively managed. The influence of stakeholders must be considered right at the start of the project when preparing the business case.

7.1.1 Typical Stakeholders

- Resources needed for the project
- People and Organisations who may be affected by the project
- People and Organisations not directly affected but who may have strong opinions about the project, either positive or negative
- Statutory and regulatory bodies
- Potential end users of the project products

End users are important stakeholders and their requirements must be captured early on when considering project requirements. It is also particularly important to recognise and manage negative stakeholders as if left unmanaged they can have a detrimental effect on the project.

The above list is not exhaustive. Each project will have its own particular set of stakeholders.

7.2 The Stakeholder Management Process

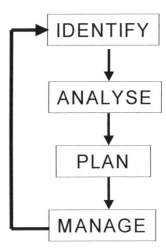

The figure opposite outlines the Stakeholder Management process.

Figure 7.1 The Stakeholder Management process

7.2.1 Identification

The most usual method of identification is by *Brainstorming.* Potential stakeholders may include:

- People affected by the project
- People on the sidelines who may have strong feelings about the project; both positive and negative.
- Statutory and regulatory bodies
- Resource requirements

Relationships between stakeholders can be represented by a Stakeholder Map such as the example shown below which relates to an IT project in a manufacturing environment.

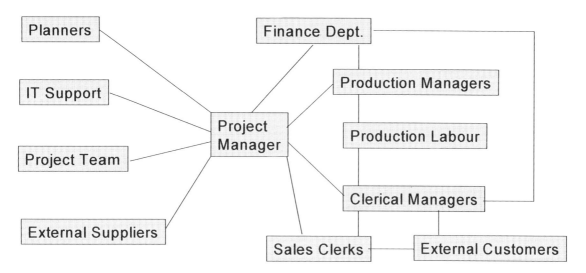

Figure 7.2 Stakeholder Map

7.2.2 Analysis

In the analysis stage it is necessary to try and discover the position of stakeholders with respect to the project. Consideration might be given to questions such as the following:

- Will they benefit from the success of the project?
- Will they be openly supportive of the project?
- Do they have reasons for wanting the project to fail?
- If their views are negative or ambivalent can they be persuaded to change?
- What is their level of power and influence?

Information can be summarized using the model shown below in figure 7.3

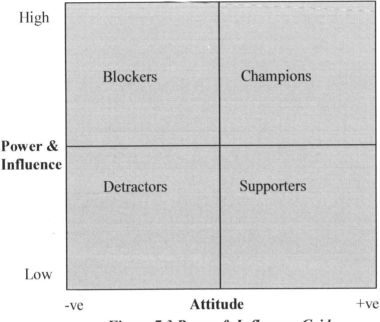

Figure 7.3 Power & Influence Grid

> **Champions** are powerful people who are actively supportive of the project.

> **Blockers** are powerful people who will actively resist the project.

> **Supporters** are people with little power who are in favour of the project.

> **Detractors** are people with little power who are against the project.

Bear in mind that Detractors and Supporters can organise themselves into focus groups and become Blockers and Champions respectively.

7.2.3 Planning

Planning consists of examining each stakeholder, trying to understand what is their likely attitude to the project, what motivates them what power they exert and then formulating an action strategy to manage and influence them. A brief example based on the project of figure 7.2 is shown in the table opposite.

Stakeholder	Attitude	Motivation	Actions
Production Manager	Champion	Success will increase productivity	Regular communication
Production Operatives	Blockers	Possible job losses	Negotiate severance pay and productivity bonus
Sales Clerks	Detractors	Think it will make their job harder	Involve in requirements and acceptance
IT Maintenance	Supporters	New system easier to maintain	Keep onside by regular updates & consultation

Figure 7.4 Stakeholder Action Plan

7.2.4 Managing

Stakeholders must be actively managed, especially as their views and motivation may change over the life of the project. The analysis must be repeated throughout the project lifecycle as new stakeholders appear and attitudes change. "Champions" can be used to managing or influencing "Blockers" or to organise "Supporters"

Another key management tool for managing stakeholders is the Communications Plan. This is covered in Chapter 17.

7.3 Benefits of Stakeholder Management

➢ Helps identify project risks and opportunities

➢ Facilitates pro-active mode of operation

➢ Facilitates managing stakeholder expectations

➢ Facilitates better working relationships

➢ Increases confidence of Stakeholders in Project Manager

➢ Increases likelihood of project success

8 Success & Benefits Management & Requirements Management

Learning Objectives

• Describe a Requirements Management process and understand the importance of effective Requirements Management

• Understand Success Criteria, Success Factors, Key Performance Indicators and how they relate to each other

•Describe Benefits Management

APMP syllabus topic 2.1, 4.1

8.1 Defining Project Requirements

A Requirements Specification is a statement, in a natural language, of what user services the system is expected to provide. It should be written so that it is understandable by the client and contractor management and by potential users. In order to correctly scope the project it is obviously of vital importance that correct requirements are obtained. However it is a common feature of SW projects in particular that what is delivered is often not what is required.

One of the best ways to ensure the quality of any project is to get the requirements for it right. If the requirements are not clearly and completely set out, any project or design based on them cannot succeed. Getting the requirements right at an early stage will prevent escalation of costs due to rework, client dissatisfaction and excessive changes during project execution and subsequent maintenance.

Requirements are about **what** is required and not about **how** they will be achieved. During the *Concept* phase high level requirements are gathered and they will be subsequently developed and revised during the *Definition* phase and beyond.

8.1.1 Benefits of a Formal Requirements Analysis Process

1. Clear definition and agreement of what stakeholders/end users require from a project will reduce future change requests that arise from incomplete requirements. Getting it right first time will greatly help to minimise deviations from the plan.

2. It facilitates change control by providing a baseline of signed-off and agreed requirements, and reduces likelihood of major changes arising. Hence, this clear baseline aids the assessment of proposed changes.

3. Having all the requirements identified up front enables then to be prioritised and thus focus on the most important requirements and not be distracted by other less important or nice to have requirements.

4. A clear handover and acceptance process can be defined and laid out from early on in project, based on complete and agreed requirements. This will provide unambiguous acceptance criteria to test and verify against.

5. It provides a clear view of what the project needs to deliver thus facilitating more robust plans which reduce the risk to the project schedule and budget, and also increases stakeholder confidence in the project.

8.2 The Requirements Process

The requirements are the foundation on which the project is built so it is essential that they are gathered in a controlled and formal manner. This is essentially a four step process:-

8.2.1 Capture

Requirements are captured mainly by interviewing relevant stakeholders. It is necessary to gain a wide spectrum of opinions to make sure that all possible requirements are captured.

8.2.2 Analysis

The gathered requirements must be tested for feasibility, validity, compatibility, acceptability, applicability and consistency. It is often found that some of the requirements of different stakeholders are mutually exclusive or are very difficult to provide. All such issues must be cleared before finalising the requirements. If necessary the Sponsor must act as referee.

8.2.3 Prioritise

It is often not possible to include all the requirements into time and budget constraints. It is therefore usual to prioritise the requirements and exclude some of them from the project scope. Here again the Sponsor may have to referee.

8.2.4 Acceptance Tests

Once the requirements have been agreed acceptance rests must be devised and agreed. They are best done at this stage rather than at completion because they clarify understanding of the requirements and will often cause them to be modified. Acceptance tests are best devised by potential end users under the guidance of the project team.

8.3 The Functional Specification

Requirements are documented in a Functional Specification. This document captures all the agreed user requirements in an unambiguous manner. It defines *what* is required but not *how* the requirement will be met. As its name implies it describes the functions of the system.

Requirements typically evolve over the life of a project. (*This is sometimes called Progressive Elaboration*) The Functional Specification is therefore a living document that is subject to *Change Control* and *Configuration Management. (See chapter 15)*

Each defined function will have an appropriate acceptance test for that function. The Functional Specification will also specify appropriate quality parameters e.g performance requirements.

8.4 Success and Benefits Management

8.4.1 Project Success Criteria

Defined by APM as "*The qualitative or quantitative criteria by which the success of a project is judged*". Possible examples are:-

- ➢ Delivered within Time & Budget tolerance
- ➢ Delivered to Specification
- ➢ Customer Satisfaction rating achieved
- ➢ Health & Safety adhered to
- ➢ Business Benefits realised
- ➢ Increased market share
- ➢ Improved productivity

From the point of view of the Project Manager success may be defined as delivering to time cost and specification. However other stakeholders may be more concerned with business benefits. These will not be known at time of handover. It is perfectly possible for a project to be deemed a delivery success but fail to produce its business benefits. On the other hand many projects delivered late and over budget have nevertheless delivered considerable business benefits.

8.4.2 Project Success Factors

Project Success Factors are those elements within the structure and context of the project that are conducive to success. These elements can be compared to *Hygiene Factors* (see paragraph 20.3.2) in that their presence will not guarantee success but their absence will markedly increase the probability of failure.

Examples are:-

- ➢ Clear project mission
- ➢ Top management support
- ➢ Client consultation
- ➢ Committed project personnel
- ➢ Monitoring and feedback mechanisms
- ➢ Clear communications
- ➢ Adequate resources

8.4.3 Key Performance Indicators

Key Performance Indicators are continuously measured over the life of the project. They directly measure the project performance against Project Success Criteria. Although success criteria can be qualitative or quantitative ideally they should be SMART. i.e.

- ➤ Specific
- ➤ Measurable
- ➤ Accountable
- ➤ Realistic
- ➤ Timely

8.5 Benefits Management

8.5.1 Responsibility

Benefits Management consists of defining the expected business benefits of a project and then monitoring the situation to ensure those benefits are delivered. The benefits of a project are rarely realised at handover and it can take weeks or months before some benefits appear. e.g productivity gains. Although on some occasions the project manager may maintain a little involvement it is generally the Sponsor who has prime responsibility for delivering business benefits.

8.5.2 Benefits review

The benefits review typically takes place 6-12 months after handover or when the "solution" has bedded in. The review will be chaired by the Project Sponsor. The people present will be mainly operational although appropriate project personnel may be present.

The review considers all the forecasted benefits of the project and compares them with the outcome. If the benefits are not forthcoming then the reasons are determined and an action plan formulated. Further benefits reviews may be necessary.

8.6 Project Failure

Very few projects can claim to have met all of their success criteria and hence, at least technically, can be said to have failed. There are many reasons why projects fail. Following are some of the more common reasons:-

- ➤ Lack of end user involvement
- ➤ Poor requirements definition
- ➤ Insufficient planning
- ➤ Lack of Risk planning and management
- ➤ Poor monitoring & Control
- ➤ Poor delegation

- ➢ High staff turnover
- ➢ Lack of sponsorship
- ➢ Poor estimating
- ➢ Poor change control
- ➢ Wrong technology
- ➢ Poor development environment
- ➢ Lack of control of 3rd parties
- ➢ Poor project management

All of these reasons can be reversed to generate success factors.

9 The Project Management Plan

Learning Objectives

- Explain the purpose, benefits and content of a typical Project Management Plan

- Describe the Authorship, Ownership and Audience of a Project Management Plan

APMP syllabus topic 2.4

9.1 The Purpose of the Project Management Plan

The Project Management Plan documents the planning outcomes of the project and provides the reference point for managing the project. It is the primary document that communicates the project manager's intentions to the Stakeholders. It is owned by the Project Manager and approved by the Sponsor. Although the project manager is responsible for its production it has to be a team activity. As well as ensuring a more robust and accurate plan it also fosters team commitment.

The plan must address seven fundamental questions.

9.1.1 The "Why"

This is developed in the Business Case. It describes the need or problem being addressed and why it is necessary to do so.

9.1.2 The "What"

This describes the scope of the project in terms of what exactly what is to be delivered. It will also describe the success criteria and the key performance indicators.

9.1.3 The "How"

This describes the project strategy including the tools and techniques to be used, the monitoring and controlling processes and reporting arrangements. It will also cover fundamental decisions such as choice of methodology, life cycle and use of third parties.

9.1.4 The "Who"

This describes project roles and responsibilities, organisational structures and plans for human resource acquisition.

9.1.5 The "When"

This documents the project schedule including key milestones.

9.1.6 The "Where"

This describes the geographical locations where the work will be carried out

9.1.7 The "How Much"

This states the project budget with expected spending by time period and by phase.

The Project Management Plan is a live, configuration controlled document which builds upon the information contained in the Business Plan. It provides a contract between the Sponsor and the Project Manager. It is a reference point for reviews, audits and control. It also assists effective handover in the event of a change in project management or sponsorship. It is the primary tool for Stakeholder communication.

9.2 Benefits of Planning

The following are the key benefits that derive from having a well thought out plan:-

- ➤ Careful consideration of project scope avoids missing things out
- ➤ Problems are anticipated and management is proactive rather than reactive
- ➤ Improves understanding - clarifies the real issues
- ➤ Concentrates attention on the deliverables
- ➤ Provides a basis for monitoring and control of budget and schedule
- ➤ Builds commitment in the team through involvement
- ➤ Improves confidence and morale of the team and stakeholders
- ➤ Establishes achievable targets and milestones
- ➤ Identifies resources required
- ➤ Establishes responsibilities
- ➤ Dramatically increases the probability of a successful project

9.3 Project Plan Content

As well as the items described above the PMP will document policies and procedures for managing aspects of the project. i.e.

- ➤ Quality Management Plan
- ➤ Change Management Plan
- ➤ Risk Management Plan
- ➤ Communications Management Plan
- ➤ Procurement Management Plan
- ➤ Health & Safety Plan
- ➤ Stakeholder Management Plan
- ➤ Environmental Impact Analysis

All of these are addressed in other sections of this document.

The Project Management Plan is unlikely to exist as a single hardcopy document. In order to be effectively maintained and be accessible to team members and appropriate stakeholders it is better to have an electronic document that is made available on the organisation's intranet.

9.4 Ownership, Authorship and Readership

Ownership

> ➤ The PM owns the responsibility for creating and maintaining the plan

> ➤ The Sponsor approves the plan and has ultimate responsibility for it

> ➤ To be motivated the Project Team must feel ownership and involvement

> ➤ Major Stakeholders must also "buy in" to the plan

Authorship

> ➤ The PM is the overall author of the PMP. However some subsections may be written by specialist team members e.g. Quality Plan, Procurement Plan

Readership

> ➤ The PMP is intended to be read by any legitimate stakeholder. e.g Sponsor and Board, Team members, Major suppliers, End Users

> ➤ It is the primary tool for Stakeholder communication

10 Scope Management

Learning Objectives

• Define project scope and scope management

• Describe the main breakdown structures used on projects (PBS, WBS, OBS, and CBS)

• Describe the purpose and use of the responsibility matrix

APMP syllabus topic 3.1

10.1 Definition

Scope Management is concerned with all the tools and processes that ensure that enough work, but no more, is carried out to produce the project deliverables. It is concerned with controlling the boundaries of the project and ensuring that all work done is related to project objectives and that any new work is subject to a formal change control process. It is also important to clearly establish what is excluded from the project scope.

The Business Plan will define the breadth of the project scope. As the project progresses the depth of the scope will increase. Scope creep and uncontrolled change are common causes of project failure so if changes are made to the scope breadth then this must be done through a formal change control process.

The primary tools for defining and controlling project scope are the Work Breakdown Structure (WBS) and the Product Breakdown Structure (PBS)

10.2 Work Breakdown Structure

The WBS is an activity based decomposition of the work to be carried out. The project is broken down level by level. The lowest levels are called work packages or tasks depending on the methodology used. Each task/work package (apart from management products) has a defined end product with an associated acceptance test to determine when it is complete. As the WBS contains all the work of the project required to produce the project deliverables it totally defines the project scope.

The WBS is the framework on which the project is built. It is not possible to build a realistic project plan without first developing a WBS that details all the project tasks that must be accomplished. The process of creating the WBS causes the project manager and all involved with the planning process to carefully consider all aspects of the project.

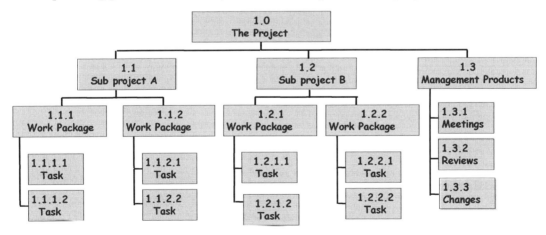

Figure 10.1 Work Breakdown Structure

The WBS shows how each work package contributes to the overall project objectives and so provides a firm basis for both planning and controlling the project. Each work package or task represents the level at which the project manager exerts control. Each WP/task is a self-contained piece of work that can be given to a single person or a small team. Each will have a list of defines attributes:-

- ➢ Specification

- ➢ Acceptance criteria

- ➢ Responsibility

- ➢ Budget

- ➢ Duration

- ➢ Resource requirements

- ➢ Dependencies

The size of these Work Packages is very important because they must be small enough to allow realistic estimates to be made, but also not so small that the sheer number of tasks overwhelms the planning and control process.

10.2.1   Benefits of the WBS
- ➢ Its production facilitates team building
- ➢ It focuses attention on project objectives
- ➢ It forces detailed planning
- ➢ It facilitates the allocation of responsibility for individual packets of work
- ➢ It graphically illustrates project scope
- ➢ It facilitates rolling-wave planning (see paragraph 5.3)
- ➢ It is the starting point for:
  - o Budgeting
  - o Estimating
  - o Scheduling
  - o Controlling
  - o Change Control
  - o Configuration Management

10.3 The Product Breakdown Structure

Whereas the WBS is activity related the PBS is product related. It breaks the project down into its constituent products and sub products as illustrated on the next page.

Production of the PBS has 3 main objectives:-

> To identify customer products

> To identify additional products which will facilitate building and supporting these products

> To gain consensus on sensible product groupings

The topmost product is the "final" product or project outcome. The PBS includes as lower level items, products supplied by external sources. Each higher level product is completely defined by the levels below. The PBS will generally include "intermediate" or "enabling" products or "sub-assemblies"

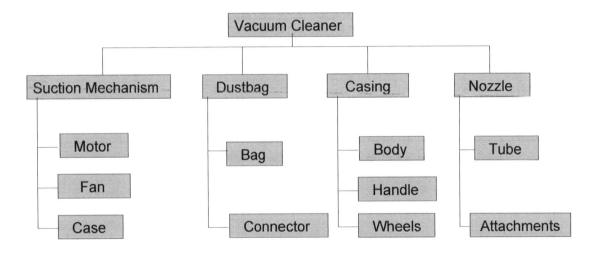

Figure 10.2 Product Breakdown Structure

10.4 Relationship between WBS and PBS

The WBS breaks down the work into individual tasks and each task delivers a "product". The PBS breaks down the product into individual components and each component requires "work". Hence the WBS and PBS are just opposite sides of the same coin; the same solution from a different viewpoint. It is also common to have hybrid situations where a product is broken down into the work needed to produce it. An example is shown opposite.

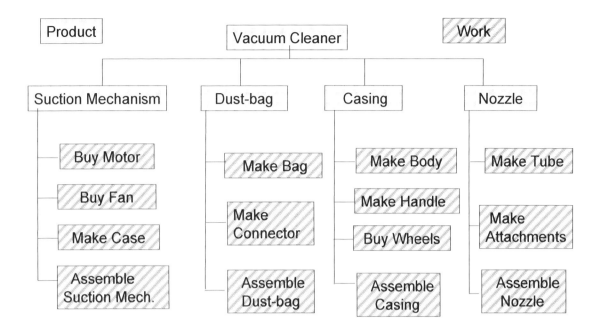

Figure 10.3 Hybrid PBS/WBS

10.5 Cost Breakdown Structure

A CBS shows all the different cost categories that make up the total project costs. The costs are applied to every work package/task on the WBS or end items on the PBS enabling costs to be rolled up to any required level. An example is shown below.

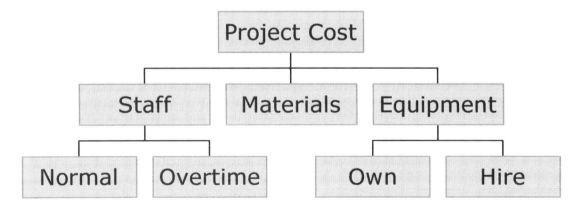

Figure 10.4 Cost Breakdown Structure

10.6 Organisational Breakdown Structure (OBS)

The OBS shows how the project team is organised. A simple example is shown below but more complicated structure can be developed to show how the project team structure relates to the structure of the organisation and communication and reporting lines.

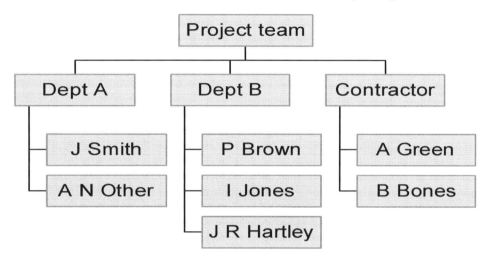

Figure 10.5 Organisational Breakdown Structure

10.7 Responsibility Assignment Matrix (RAM)

The WBS and OBS can be combined to produce a matrix which shows the personnel required to execute each work package/task.

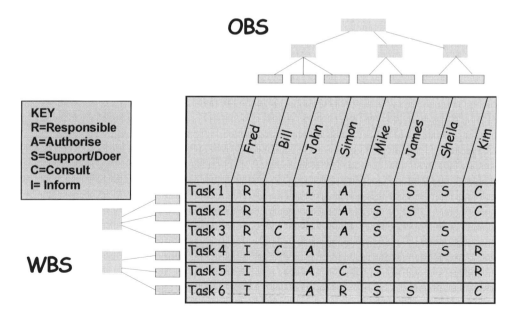

Figure 10.6 Responsibility Assignment Matrix

11 Estimating

Learning Objectives

•Understand the problems of estimating across the project life cycle

•Understand:-

 –Bottom Up Estimating
 –Comparative Estimating
 –Parametric Estimating
 –Three Point Estimating

APMP syllabus topic 4.3

11.1 Estimating Methods

An estimate is a quantified assessment of the resources required to complete part or all of the project. It is stated in terms of cost & time & resources. Inaccurate (usually over optimistic) estimating is a major cause of project failure. Some would say it is **the** major cause. Estimates must initially be made at Business Plan stage. These estimates are usually based on high level data but people are often very reluctant to revise them even when experience is showing that they are wrong. It is essential in any project for outcomes to be compared to initial estimates and estimates adjusted if necessary, even if these causes the business plan to be re-examined.

There are four main estimating methods

1. Bottom Up Estimating
2. Comparative Estimating
3. Parametric Estimating
4. Three Point Estimating

These 4 methods can be used independently but more usually in combination.

11.1.1   Bottom Up Estimating

This method is based on the WBS. All the individual lower level tasks in the WBS are estimated independently and then rolled up to produce the project estimates. This is a laborious method and its accuracy is dependant on having a correct WBS. However it is the most accurate way of estimating. It is sometimes known as the definitive estimate. The aimed for accuracy is to be within 5%.

11.1.2   Comparative Estimating

This is also called Top Down or Historic estimating. It simply involves using experience from similar projects carried out in the past. It takes the overall costs and timescales for similar projects and adjusts them for size and complexity. The danger is that previous projects may have been inefficient and/or badly managed. Comparative estimating can also be used at task level to support bottom up.

11.1.3   Parametric Estimating

Parametric estimating uses a mathematical model or formulae to produce project estimates based on input parameters. It is usually based on historical data. Simple examples are square metres in construction and lines of code in software development. Quantity Surveyors make extensive use of parametric estimating. More complex software applications such as COCOMO and Function Point Analysis are beyond the scope of this course.

11.1.4 Three Point Estimating

All the above methods are single point estimates. We normally recognise their inherent inaccuracy by adding on a contingency allowance. Three point estimating recognises the uncertainty in the estimating process and attempts, for each estimate, to set upper and lower bounds as well as a most likely value. This is illustrated below.

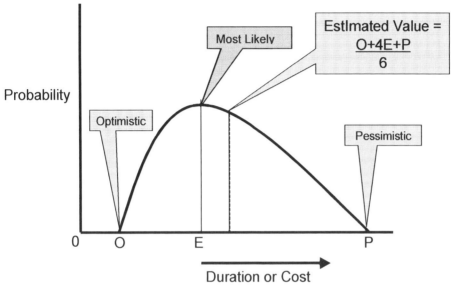

Figure 11.1 Three Point Estimating

Instead of developing a single estimate we estimate a best possible "optimistic" time, the highest likely "pessimistic" time, worst case scenario, and what is believed to be the "expected" or best estimate. Experience has shown that by asking for 3 estimates rather than 1 the expected value obtained is a better estimate than just asking for a single value. The distribution is generally skewed to the right as shown above. This means that the new "Estimated Value" will be higher than the "Most Likely" value. Thus the resulting schedule is more pessimistic, and hence usually more realistic.

Most software packages that we use to calculate a schedule will only accept a single value. A single estimate is calculated from the formulae:-

Estimated Value = (Optimistic + 4*Expected + Pessimistic)/6

This is called a "heuristic" or "rule of thumb" and has been found to give good results in practice. Note that because of the inherently skewed nature of the distribution towards the left, the estimated value will always be higher than the original expected value.

This is sometimes referred to as a PERT estimate. See paragraph 12.2

There are some software packages which take as input all three parameters and produce as output a probability distribution on time and budget. This is known as **Monte Carlo Simulation.** This topic is beyond the scope of this text.

11.2 The Estimating Funnel

Estimates cost time and money to produce and the more accuracy required the more expense involved. The estimating process typically goes through 5 stages where each estimate is used to justify the effort of producing the next one. The stages are:

	% Accuracy
1. Proposal	-30 to +50
2. Budget	-20 to +35
3. Sanction	-10 to +25
4. Control	-5 to +15
5. Tender	-2 to + 5

We recognise the inaccuracies in the early stages of estimating by applying appropriate contingency allowances. As the project develops and additional information is obtained the accuracy improves and contingencies can be reduced.

The way in which accuracy improves over the project lifecycle can be seen in the "Estimating Funnel" illustrated below.

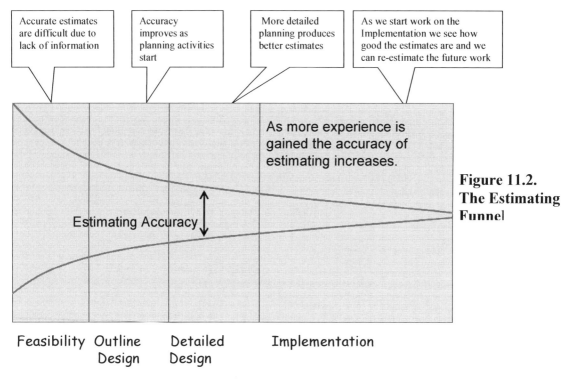

Figure 11.2. The Estimating Funnel

12 Scheduling & Resource Management

Learning Objectives

• Explain how a schedule is created and maintained and understand the following concepts:-

  –Precedence diagrams
  –Critical path
  –Total float and free float
  –Gantt charts
  –Duration estimating including PERT
  –Milestone planning

• Understand the use of software scheduling tools

• Understand resource management

• Understand resource smoothing (time limited scheduling)

• Understand resource levelling (resource limited scheduling)

APMP syllabus topics 3.2, 3.3

12.1 The Precedence Diagramming Method

There are two distinct methods by which activities can be scheduled. Historically the first method was called the "Activity on Arrow" method where each task to be scheduled is represented by an arrow and the arrows are logically linked to form a network. This method has now been largely superseded by the "Activity on Node" or "Precedence Diagramming Method" (PDM) which is the one used by the vast majority of software packages.

In the Precedence Diagramming Method tasks are represented by boxes with dependencies shown as logical connections between the boxes. A simple example is shown below.

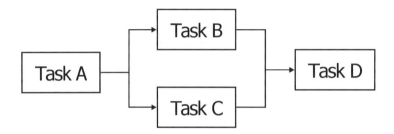

 Upon completion of Task A we can start Tasks B and C. Once both these are completed we can start task D. Thus B and C are preceded by A and D is preceded by B and C.

The tasks are derived from the WBS. Each box represents a lowest level task or work package.

12.1.1   Other Link Types with Leads and Lags

The relationship described above (finish to start) is the one most commonly used but there are three other possible relationships making four in all.

1. Start to Start
B can start 2 days after A starts

2. Finish to Finish
D can not finish until 3 days after C finishes

3. Start to Finish
F cannot finish until at least 4 days after E starts

4. Finish to Start
There is at least 1 day between G finishing and H starting.

Leads and lags
 Leads originate from start times and lags from finish times.

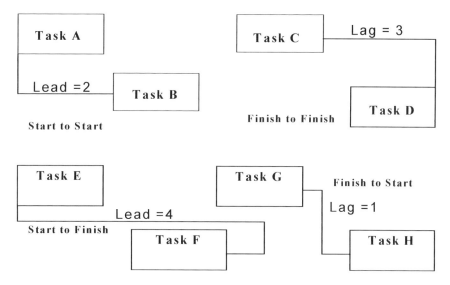

Figure 12.1 Precedence Relationships

12.1.2   Critical Path Analysis (CPA)

Critical path analysis comprises 3 steps.

1) The Forward Pass – from left to right

This pass calculates the earliest possible start and finish times for each task.

Early Finish = Early Start + Duration

2) The Backward Pass – from right to left

This pass calculates the latest possible start and finish dates which will complete the schedule on time.

Late Start = Late Finish - Duration.

3) Calculate Total Float

Total Float = Late Finish – Early Finish or Late Start – Early Start

Total Float is defined as the amount of time an activity can be delayed or extended without affecting the total project duration (end date)

12.1.3   Node Convention

ES	Dur.	EF
ID Description		
LS	TF	LF

ES = Earliest Start Time
Dur = Activity Duration
EF = Earliest Finish Time
LS = Latest Start Time
TF = Total Float
LF = Latest Finish Time

12.1.4   Worked Example

Draw and completely analyse an activity-on-node network for the following project, assuming the project is to be completed in minimum time.

Activity	Duration	Dependency
A	10	NONE
B	15	A
C	5	A
D	8	A
E	2	D
F	10	B,C,E

Step 1- Construct the network and enter the durations

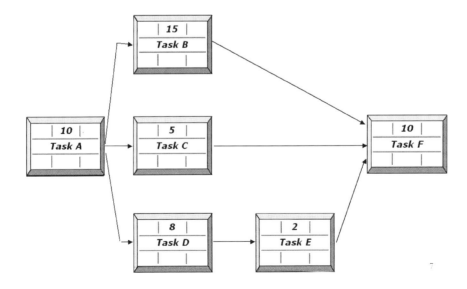

Figure 12.2

Step 2- Carry out the forward pass

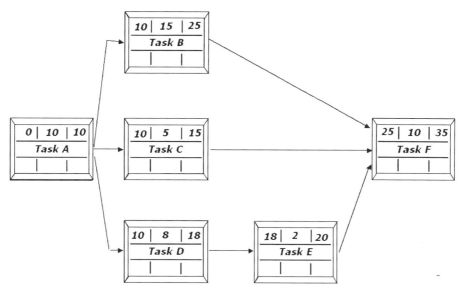

Figure 12.3

Thus for activity A, 0 + 10 = 10. This 10 is carried forward to all the successor activities and so on. Where there are multiple arrows we take the latest (the largest) as before. Thus for activity F we take the largest of 25 (from B), 15(from C) and 20(from E).

Step 3- Carry out the backward pass

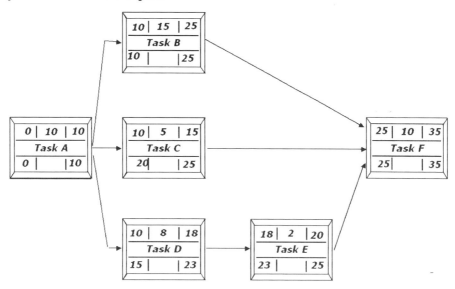

Figure 12.4

Thus for activity F,   35(the finish time) – 10 (duration) = 25 (the start time)
This 25 becomes the latest finish date for B, C and E

Where there are multiple backward arrows e.g into activity A then we take the smallest which in this case is the 10 from B.

Step 4 Calculate Total Float by subtracting the early dates from the late dates.

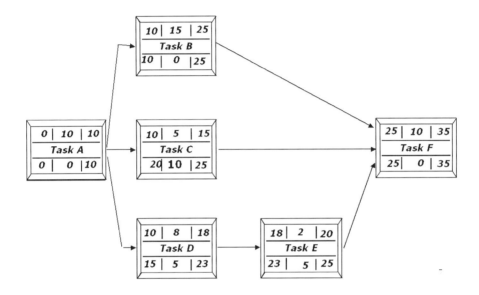

Figure 12.5

12.1.5   The Critical Path

The Critical path is the sequence of activities through a project network from start to finish, the sum of whose durations determines the overall project duration. On this path the late completion of activities will have an impact on the project end date.

The Critical Path is:-
> ➢ The longest path through the network
> ➢ The shortest possible planned project duration
> ➢ The path with least float

Thus in the above example the critical path is A>B>F

Knowledge of the Critical Path assists in the following areas:-

> ➢ To concentrate attention on activities which, if delayed, will affect project duration
> ➢ To identify non-critical activities which can be used to smooth forecast resource usage

- To identify 'near or sub critical' activities - those with very little float which require similar attention to critical activities
- To identify where resources can be switched between activities to maintain progress

12.1.6 Free Float

Total Float is defined as the amount of time a task can be delayed without delaying the end date. **Free Float** is defined as the amount of time an activity can be delayed or extended without delaying the start of the next activity. The presence or absence of free float can be determined by inspection as the following example shows.

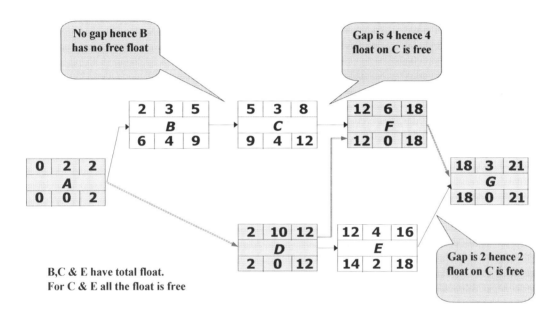

Figure 12.6 Free Float

The significance of Free Float is that the project manager knows that he can utilise free float to for instance ease temporary resource problems, knowing that there are no knock on effects. If there is total float but no free float then there will be knock on effects to consider. Also note that where a sequence of tasks in a line such as B,C above exhibit a value for total float then that float is effectively shared. If we utilise some or all of the total float in B then it will be removed from C.

12.1.7 Crashing and Fast Tracking

When projects fall behind schedule there are two techniques, which can be used in an attempt to get back on time. They are **crashing** and **fast tracking**

Crashing involves adding more resources to activities that are on the critical path in order to reduce the elapsed time of those activities. Here are some important guidelines:

1) Focus on activities on the critical path
2) Choose activities that are indeed "crashable" (adding resources to some late tasks may only make them even later)
3) Focus first on the activities in which the cost of crashing is lowest

Crashing the network invariably increases project costs

Fast tracking involves doing more activities in parallel, that is, trying to create more parallel paths. Both Fast Tracking and Crashing require more concentrated resources. This approach usually increases risk.

12.2 P.E.R.T

PERT stands for **Program Evaluation and Review Technique.** This model was invented by Booz Allen Hamilton, Inc. under contract to the Defence's US Navy Special Projects Office in 1958 as part of the Polaris ballistic missile project. Basically it was a marriage of the Activity on Arrow method mentioned in 12.1 with the 3 point estimating method discussed in 11.1.4. The 3 point estimating method is often referred to as a PERT estimate and the weighted average formulae as the PERT formulae.

12.3 Gantt Charts

Strictly speaking a Gantt is just a series of bars, representing activities against a timeline which shows when activities take place. However the original concept has been extended to include logical connections which effectively means it is a network with the boxes drawn to a time scale. The figure below shows an example of a software generated Gantt chart.

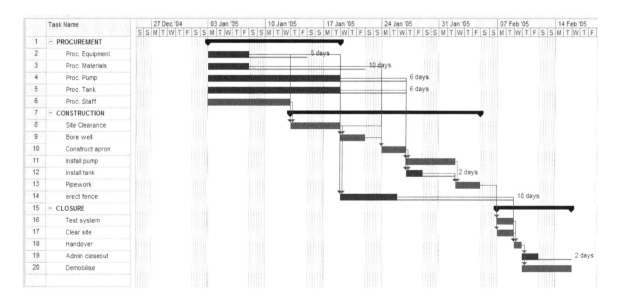

Figure 12.7 Software generated Gantt chart

12.3.1   Gantt Chart Features

Gantt charts are the most common way of representing a project schedule. They exhibit the following features

- ➤ A timeline shows the project calendar
- ➤ The length of a bar indicates duration
- ➤ Tasks are usually positioned at the earliest start date showing any float at the end
- ➤ Can be shown with or without logic connections (technically speaking a true Gantt chart does not show logical connections)
- ➤ Can also show comparison of current plan to original plan (baseline)
- ➤ Can be rolled up into summary tasks and can show milestones (key events, moments in time)
- ➤ Can be generated using software tools
- ➤ They are often simply referred to as Bar Charts

12.3.2   Gantt v Network

The following figure shows how a Gantt chart and a Precedence Network are effectively two ways of depicting the same situation.

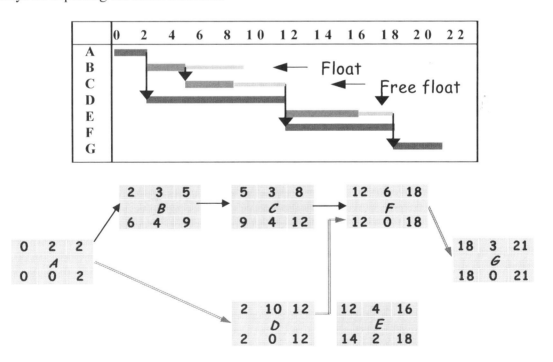

Figure 12.8 Comparison of Gantt and Network

12.4 Milestone Planning

Although it is usually necessary to plan in detail, in the early stages of a project such detail is not usually available and planning takes place at a less detailed level. We generally start by establishing the key milestones. Milestones are key occurrences in the project which mark the achievement of key objectives such as the completion of a phase. Milestones are used by management for project control. They are often not concerned with project detail but only in the progress against key milestones. Milestones are often linked to payment schedules. Completion of a milestone can trigger the issuing of an invoice.

A plan which shows only high level activities and major milestones is known as a Project Master Schedule

An extremely useful tool for controlling projects at milestone level is the Milestone Progress Chart (often erroneously called a Milestone Slip Chart) shown below.

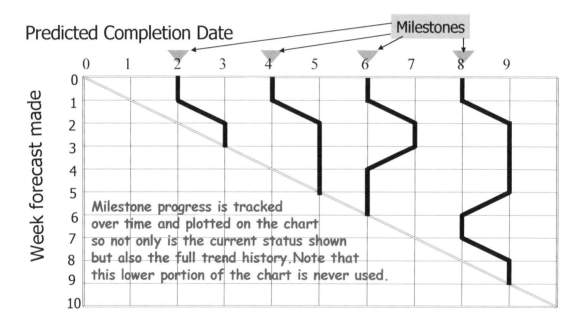

Figure 12.9 Milestone Progress Chart

Progress according to plan is indicated by a vertical line. A line parallel to the diagonal indicates no progress. A milestone is complete when the diagonal is reached.

This is a very simple and powerful tool for reporting progress to management.
Not only does it show the current state of all the milestones it also shows the complete history and the trends.

12.5 Use of Software Tools

Scheduling, using networks or Gantt charts can be a laborious process and for large projects maintaining them becomes an impossible task. For at but the simplest projects we tend to use a software tool. This has many advantages:-

- ➢ The schedule is easier to maintain
- ➢ We can easily show the current status against the original baseline plan
- ➢ It can be automatically integrated with resource planning and earned value
- ➢ It provides electronic storage, distribution and access
- ➢ Has good reporting facilities
- ➢ Automatically calculates critical path, float and resource profiles and cost information
- ➢ Automatically handles calendar issues such as non working days and shutdowns
- ➢ Can simulate different what-if scenarios

There are some drawbacks. Many packages are extremely sophisticated and need a long learning curve. It is often hard to understand what the software is doing. It can provide a false sense of security as most packages assume the future is always on plan.

12.6 Resource Management

Resource Management is concerned mainly with people but also includes all project resources such as money and raw materials.

There are two principal classes of resources used on projects.

1) Consumables (Replenishable)
   These can only be used once and must then be replenished. Examples include raw materials and money.
2) Re-usable
   Once no longer needed they are available for use elsewhere. Examples include machines, tools and of course people.

Resource Management is concerned with making resources available when required and avoiding waste. In the case of people it is better to have a smooth profile rather than continuous hire and fire. There are two methods for achieving this.

1) Time Limited Scheduling (Smoothing)

This is usually the default option. Scheduling of resources will take place ignoring resource constraints. In other words infinite resource is assumed. This is usually the default option when doing the initial planning.

2) Resource Limited Scheduling (Levelling)

No time limit is placed on the schedule. Tasks will take place at the earliest times resources become available.

12.7 Resource Smoothing

Resource smoothing attempts to resolve resource overloads by utilising Float. In this example utilising the float on activities C and E will not totally resolve the problem.

Consider the example here.

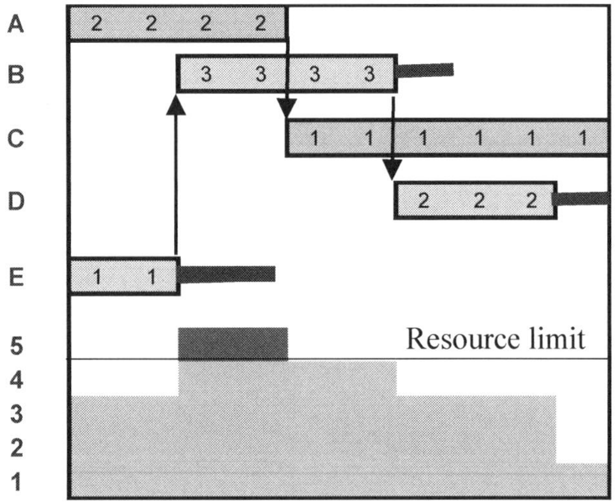

Figure 12.10
Resource Smoothing.
Starting point

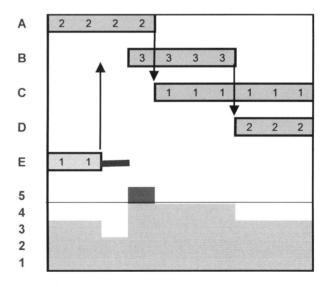

Applying **Resource Smoothing** and utilising the **float** on activity B and D we arrive at the position below. This is a **Time constrained schedule**. Here the network schedule is allowed to change but the end date is retained. ***Resource Smoothing*** *is time constrained.*

Time constrained schedule

In this case the network schedule is fixed and the program will allocate the required resource.

Figure 12.11
Resource Smoothing.
Finishing point

12.8 Resource Levelling

In order to fully address the resource overload, in this example we must delay B and hence D thus extending the project. This process of **Resource Levelling** is resource constrained and the outcome is shown below.

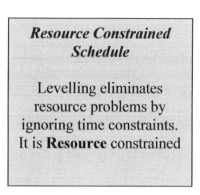

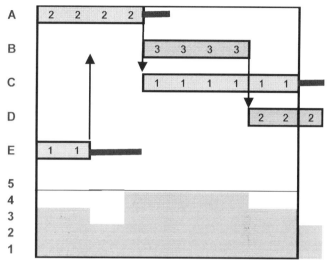

Figure 12.13 Resource Levelling

12.9 Software Tools

Software tools can automate resource planning calculations. However they need to be told which scheduling method and resource allocation rules to use. They also support more sophisticated scenarios e.g

➤ Relationship between resource amount and task duration
➤ The ability to split activities to assist in smoothing and levelling
➤ The ability to apply different resource levels over the duration of an activity.

These features are illustrated in the following example.

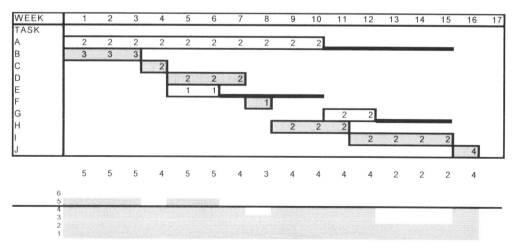

Figure 12.14 Before Smoothing

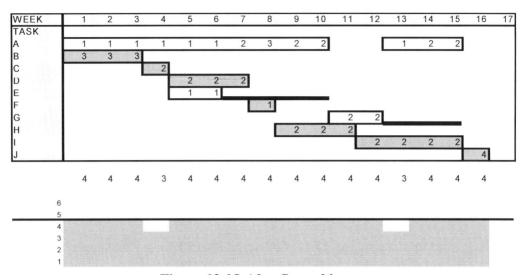

Figure 12.15 After Smoothing

 It can be seen that the resource profile has been smoothed by splitting task A and varying the resource, the assumption being, that resource is a linear function of time.

12.10   *Cost Budgeting*

Cost budgeting involves aggregating the estimated costs of all work packages over time to establish a total cost baseline for measuring project progress. The starting point for this process is the resource schedule. The cost baseline is the basis of cost control and Earned Value Management. This will be followed up in chapter 17.

13 Managing Risks and Issues

Learning Objectives

•Describe the Risk Management process

•Explain the benefits of Risk Management

•Understand the concept of risk as both a threat and an opportunity

•Understand the difference between Risks and Issues

APMP syllabus topic 2.5, 3.8

13.1 Definitions of Risk

APM definition:

"Combination of the probability or frequency of occurrence of a defined threat or opportunity and the magnitude of the consequence of the occurrence."

The above is more a statement of how risk is measured. A better definition is:-

A project risk is something that might occur, and if it does, will impact on the project's objectives of time, cost and performance/quality. Risk is uncertainty in an outcome. Risks can be both threats (downside) and opportunities (upside).

13.2 The Risk Management Plan

By their nature all projects are inherently risky; therefore the management of risk should an integral part of the project and carried out over the entire life cycle. Traditionally risks have been thought of solely as negative events but current thinking treats risk as uncertainty which can have positive or negative effects. The term "risk event" covers both threats and opportunities and both can be managed through a single process.

The way in which risk is to be managed in a project is detailed in the "**Risk Management Plan.**" The Risk Management Plan defines how all the risk processes will be carried out. It does not consider individual risks. Risk management plan content

  ➢ The methodology and data sources
  ➢ Roles & responsibilities
  ➢ Budgeting for risk management
  ➢ Timing, i.e. when risk assessment will be carried out
  ➢ Qualitative and quantitative scoring methods
  ➢ Risk thresholds
  ➢ Reporting format
  ➢ How risks will be tracked

13.3 Risk Management Process

The purpose of risk management is to identify all significant risks to the project and manage those risks so as to eliminate or minimise threats, and maximise opportunities. The process is outlined in the diagram opposite.

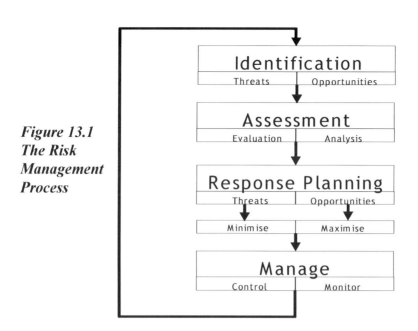

Figure 13.1
The Risk
Management
Process

The APM Body of Knowledge also identifies an Initiation Process before Identification. This step effectively replicates the production of the Risk Management Plan. The final step is referred to as Implementation. Thus the APM steps are named:-

INITIATE>IDENTIFY>ASSESS>PLAN RESPONSES>IMPLEMENT RESPONSES

13.3.1   Risk Identification

There are a variety of techniques for identification of risks events. e.g.

➢ **Brainstorming**
    Using the project team and appropriate stakeholders
➢ **SWOT Analysis**
    Strengths and Opportunities generate upside risks
    Weaknesses and Threats identify downside risks
➢ **Assumptions Analysis**
    Looking at the assumptions made in the planning to see if any of them constitute a risk
➢ **Constraints analysis**
    Similarly for project constraints
➢ **Using the WBS**
    Identifying risks to individual work packets
➢ **Interviews**
    Interviewing people with knowledge or insight

There may also be sources of information external to the project that can help the identification process e.g.

- ➤ **Prompt/Check Lists**
  - Using existing prompt sheets and check lists
- ➤ **Post Project Reviews (Lessons learned)**
  - From previous projects with some commonality
- ➤ **Risk Registers of other projects**
  - Again, using projects with some commonality

13.3.2   Risk Assessment

The purpose of Risk Assessment is to prioritise the identified risks. In particular it needs to establish the key risks that require management focus.

Assessment is based on determining Probability and Impact and this is most conveniently carried out with the aid of a Probability and Impact Grid.

13.3.2.1   Probability and Impact Grid

The Probability and Impact Grid is a simple but effective tool that is used to prioritise identified risks. An example is illustrated below. In this instance we are using a scale that involves using judgement to place probability and impact from very low to very high.

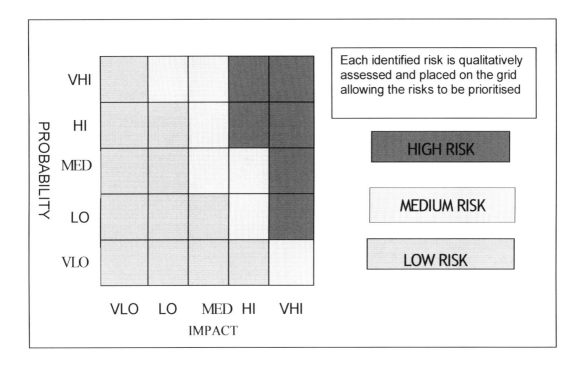

Figure 13.2 Probability and Impact Grid

13.3.2.2   Qualitative and Quantitative Analysis

The above assessment method is purely **Qualitative** in the sense that the scales are subjective assessments of the probability and impact. This is sufficient to prioritise the risks but for a full and proper assessment the analysis should be **Quantitative.** The probability grid can be converted to a quantitative method by stating probability and impact in numeric terms. There are also other quantitative techniques such as Monte Carlo methods and Decision Tree analysis but these are beyond the scope of this course.

A pseudo quantitative method often used is to simply apply a scale of 1 to 5 to the impact and probability. Multiplying these scales gives the *Exposure* for each square that can be used to prioritise the risks.

Exposure = Probability x Impact

A drawback of this method is that it gives the same weight to both probability and impact whereas in reality high impact is more serious than high probability. High impact items must be addressed even if they have low probability. The shading in the grid is a better representation of the relative importance.

5	5	10	15	20	25
4	4	8	12	16	20
3	3	6	9	12	15
2	2	4	6	8	10
1	1	2	3	4	5
	1	**2**	**3**	**4**	**5**

Figure 13.3

13.3.2.3   Benefits and features of the method

The probability and impact grid is widely used because it is a simple and effective tool that has many benefits.

> * It captures all identified risks
> * It is a good visual representation which aids communication
> * It facilitates a brainstorming approach that can provide a whole team view
> * It provides a simple way for risk prioritisation
> * Shows individual probability and impact not just exposure
> * The levels of risk identified steer us towards the most appropriate contract type
> * The method gives a basis of measuring overall magnitude of risk to the project

13.3.3   Risk Response Planning

13.3.3.1   Threats

There are 5 common strategies for addressing downside risks or threats. These are applied either individually or in combination.

1. **Avoid**
   Avoid the risk and eliminate uncertainty by not doing something or doing it in a different way
2. **Transfer**
   Transfer liability or ownership of a risk to someone else such as the client or sub-contractor or 3rd party. e.g. insurance or back to back contracts
3. **Reduce/Mitigate**
   If the risk cannot be avoided and is too large to accept then we must take steps to reduce probability and/or impact
4. **Accept**
   Take it on board and accept the consequences. The severity/probability of the risk does not justify great effort in managing it.
5. **Contingency Plan**
   Have an alternative plan at hand to implement if the risk occurs

When the severity of a risk determines that it must be actively managed then the following process should be followed:-

1. Re-examine the risk to determine its current status and validate the previous evaluation
2. Demonstrate the viability of the mitigation plan by evaluating the cost of mitigation and comparing with the reduction in exposure.
3. Decide if the mitigation results in an acceptable level of risk.
4. If so decide on who will own and manage the risk and be empowered to do so.
   For any risk the person who manages that risk should be the person best placed to do so.

13.3.3.2   Opportunities

Similarly there are strategies for developing opportunities.

1. **Exploit**
   Try and exploit the opportunity by eliminating the uncertainties surrounding the opportunity
2. **Share**
   If you do not have the resources to exploit the opportunity yourself then try to find a partner to share it.

3. **Enhance**
   Work to increase the probability and impact of the opportunity
4. **Accept**
   Wait and see what happens

13.3.4   Managing the risks

Each risk that has a planned response must be proactively managed by the person responsible. In addition the risk plan needs to be formally reviewed on a regular basis.

The situation is bound to change because:-

> Some risks mature into problems (issues)
> Some risks are resolved or do not arise
> Probability/impacts change; up or down
> New risks arise that were not identified initially
> Project scope changes give new risk opportunities

The primary tool for managing risk is the Risk Register an example of which is shown below.

Figure 13.4 Example Risk register

Project _____						Prepared by: _____		Reference:_____	
Key: H - High, M - Medium, L - Low							Date:_____		
Risk ID	Description	Prob H M L			Impact Cost Time		Response Strategy	Effect	Risk Owner

The Risk Register must be routinely reviewed on a regular basis and when risk events happen. The overall risk status of the project and the progress of "active" risks will be reported as part of the standard project reporting procedures as defined in the Risk Management Plan and the Communications Plan.

13.4 The Benefits of Managing Risk

On many projects risks are not actively managed for the reasons stated later on. However as well as being a requirement of good **Governance,** the proper management of risk confers significant benefits.

> ➤ Increased understanding by the project leads to more realistic plans and greater probability of delivering to them. Increased understanding of the risks, leads to their minimisation and allocation to the person best placed to manage them. The understanding of risk helps determine the most appropriate contract type. A team view of the risks can lead to more objective decision making

> ➤ Financially and/or technically unsound/risky projects will be discouraged There will be a better understanding of the project by Stakeholders leading to increased confidence in the Project Management. It focuses management attention on the most significant threats to the project

13.5 Drawbacks of Managing Risk

The Cost

Risk Management is an overhead requiring a significant input of effort and cost. Although this is no different from the input of effort and cost into all Planning processes, such as Scope Management and Change Control, there is one key difference - Risk Management is about things that may never happen and even if they might, "it won't happen to me".

Visibility

Once we have put lots of effort and money into Risk Management the likely result is that it tells us what we didn't want to know. We will either have to invest in reducing the risks or accept that the project might take a lot longer, or cost a lot more than we had hoped or even that we should not do the project at all.

Many people may have a vested interest in the project and do not wish to hear anything that might endanger it.

13.6 Issue Management

In the PMBOK APM define an Issue as a problem that cannot be solved by the project manger. *APM admit that this is not a generally held definition.* A more universal definition of an issue is a problem that requires immediate attention. Some issues arise out of risks events that had been previously identified. Others will come as a complete surprise.

Some Issues may necessitate formal changes that require the Change Control Process (Chapter 15) to be invoked. For example a Client suddenly announces a major budget cut which necessitates reduction to project scope.

Some Issues will not cause a formal change but must be managed. For example a key resource resigns from the project or a vital piece of equipment breaks down.

It is important to have a formal process to manage issues. If they are caught earlier they should be easier to resolve before causing damage. The process is similar to Risk management

> **Identification**
>> o By their very nature Issues tend to identify themselves
> **Escalation**
>> o At what level in the project/organisation must this issue be addressed for a solution? Who owns the issue?
> **Monitoring**
>> o The Owner monitors the issue and reports on progress. An Issue log is maintained.
> **Resolution**
>> o The issue is closed when fully resolved to the satisfaction of all parties.

Issues can be thought of as Risks that were not previously identified or were Accepted. Many organisations group risks and issues together and maintain a single Risks & Issues Log.

14 Quality Management

Learning Objectives

- Describe what is meant by project quality management

- Understand the processes of quality planning, quality control and quality assurance

- Have an understanding of common quality management techniques

- Explain the benefits of quality management

APMP syllabus topic 2.6

14.1 Definition of Quality

Quality can be defined as the totality of characteristics of an entity that bear on its ability to satisfy stated or implied needs. A quality product must conform to the defined requirements/specifications but most importantly must be "fit for purpose".

Customer requirements are the basis for managing Quality. A "Quality" product is one that meets the specification and satisfies the customer.

"Over delivering" often called "Gold Plating" can be regarded as poor quality.

14.2 Quality V Grade

Quality must not be confused with Grade. Grade is to do with relative functionality and features. A high grade product may be rich in functionality and possibly luxury fittings but if it does not conform to requirements and meet customer expectations it is not a quality product. Conversely a product with basic, minimal functionality and lack of "frills" can be a quality product.

14.3 Elements of Quality Management

Quality Management is a management discipline concerned with making sure that activities happen according to a prescribed plan. It is all about preventing problems. Quality management involves carrying out a project through all its phases with zero deviations from the project specifications and adhering to defined processes.

The elements of Project Quality Management are:-

> **Quality Planning**
> **Quality Assurance**
> **Quality Control**

14.3.1   Quality Planning

Quality planning is defined as "identifying which quality standards are relevant to the project and determining how to apply and satisfy them". In other words setting standards and how to achieve them. The primary output of the quality planning process is the Project Quality Management Plan. It describes how the project team intends to implement its Quality Policy. This reinforces the basis of modern thinking about project quality management; that is quality is a planned activity and not something that is applied afterwards by inspection and correction. Inspection still has a part to play in quality management; however increased inspection is not generally considered the best path to improved quality.

The Contents of the Quality Management Plan comprise:

➢ Project Deliverables
➢ Quality Standards
➢ Quality Systems
➢ Quality Tools,
➢ Quality Control Processes and Procedures
➢ Quality Assurance Processes and Procedures
➢ Organisation, Roles & Responsibilities
➢ Reporting Standards

14.3.2   Quality Assurance

Quality Assurance is defined as the process of evaluating overall project performance on a regular basis to provide confidence that the project will satisfy the relevant quality standards.

The following items are part of quality assurance:

Formal Audits

➢ Project Audit
➢ Quality Audit - ISO 9000
➢ Financial Audit
➢ Technical Audit

Audits examine if processes, policies and procedures are being adhered to. Audits can be internal to the project, within the organisation but outside the projects or from external bodies. e.g checking for ISO 9000 compliance.

Reviews

Reviews can be more informal than audits. Thy concentrate more on what the project is producing and the project status and environment rather than the processes. Reviews should be constructive not destructive or people will be reluctant to participate.

14.3.3   Quality Control

Quality Control involves measuring project products to test if they conform to the relevant standards and also identifying ways to correct unsatisfactory performance and deviation from specification.

14.4 Tools for Quality

Many of the tools and techniques discussed in this course have direct relevance to quality, e.g Risk Management and Configuration Management. In addition there are some specific tools that are commonly used. e.g.

- ➢ Ishikawa diagram
- ➢ Pareto Chart
- ➢ Control Chart

14.4.1   Ishikawa Diagram

Named after its inventor this tool is also known as a "Fishbone Diagram" or a "Cause and Effect Diagram". An example of its use is shown below where it is being used to investigate the causes of schedule overruns. Each primary cause, such as Installation Delays, can be broken down further into sub-causes. Each of these can then be investigated.

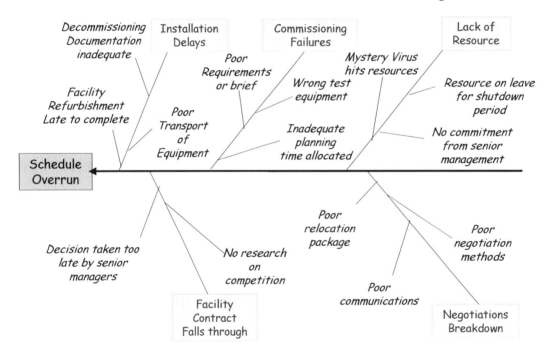

Figure 14.1 Ishikawa Diagram

14.4.2   Pareto Chart (80/20 rule)

In the 19th century an Italian economist called Vilfredo Pareto found that typically 80 percent of the wealth in a region was concentrated in less than 20 percent of the population.

This was taken up in modern times by Dr. Joseph Juran who formulated what he called the Pareto Principle. This states that in most situations only a vital few elements (about 20%) account for the majority (about 80%) of the problems that are occurring. For example take an automobile production line. It has been shown that 20% of the possible causes account for 80 %of the downtime. The practical application of the Pareto principle is that 80% of the problems can be cured by addressing only 20% of the causes.

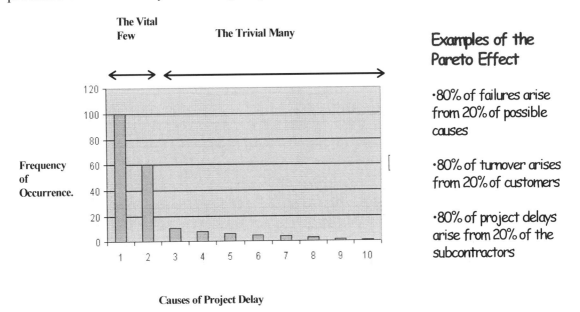

Figure 14.2 The Pareto Effect

14.4.3   Control Charts

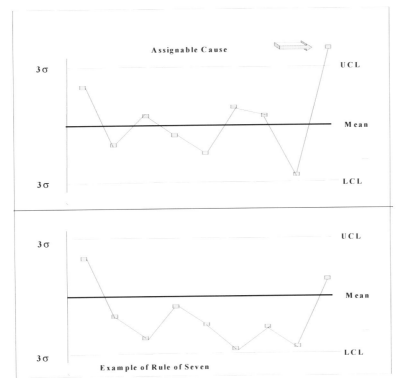

Figure 14.3 Control Chart

The centre line of the chart of figure 14.3 represents the process average or mean. The upper and lower control limits (UCL & LCL) are typically set at 3σ either side of the mean. This means that for a Normal distribution 99.7% of values will be within the control limits. Thus a value outside these limits is highly likely to indicate a problem with the process.

Control limits describe the natural variation of the process such that points within the limits are generally indicative of normal and expected variation. Points outside the limits signal that probably something has occurred that requires special attention because it is outside of the built-in systemic causes of variation in the process.

14.4.3.1   Assignable Causes

It is possible that points outside the 3σ control limits are due to random variation. However it is likely that there is an **assignable cause**, meaning that their occurrence may be the result of unwanted, external effects such as-

- ➤ An equipment problem
- ➤ An employee problem (poor training, understaffed etc)
- ➤ Defective materials

14.4.3.2   Rule of 7

This rule of thumb (heuristic) states that if seven or more observations in a row occur on the same side of the mean (even though they may be within the control limit) or if seven or more readings show a continuous upward or downward trend they should be investigated as if they had an assignable cause.

14.4.3.3   Specification Limits

The upper and lower control limits (UCL and LCL) must not be confused with specification limits. Specification limits (or tolerances) can often be more stringent than the capability of the process. It may be that for say jet engine components the tolerance may be equal to a lot less than 3 sigma. If the process can not be improved to reduce its inherent variation then a large proportion of the production will be rejected (this is the case in computer chip production). However in this instance the process is still under control if it is within control limits and obeying the rule of 7. Thus a process in control can still produce out of spec goods

14.5 Continuous Improvement and Kaizen

The Japanese word for continuous improvement is Kaizen. The philosophy espoused by kaizen is that quality comes from continuous minor improvements. It is the responsibility of both workers and management to always be on the look out for ways to improve the quality of the finished product and the processes that produce it. This also can involve "Lean Thinking" which is concerned with continuously striving to reduce resources without adversely affecting quality and this increasing productivity and profitability.

14.6 Just-in-Time (JIT) and Kanban

Kanban stands for Kan- card, Ban- signal. The essence of the Kanban concept is that a supplier or the warehouse should only deliver components to the production line as and when they are needed, i.e. *Just-in-Time*, so that there is no storage in the production area. Within this system, workstations located along production lines only produce/deliver desired components when they receive a card and an empty container, indicating that more parts will be needed in production. . Since Kanban is a chain process in which orders flow from one process to another, the production or delivery of components are pulled to the production line. In contrast to the traditional forecast oriented method where parts are pushed to the line.

When there is no safety stock in the system, defective parts or processes will result in lost production. JIT thus forces a company to find and fix quality problems before they occur.

14.7 Total Quality Management (TQM)

TQM is not a quality technique. It is a philosophy concerned with how best to achieve quality improvement within an organisation, bringing together the approached of Deming, Juran and Crosby. It is an approach that puts quality at the heart of everything that it done by the organisation. It lays particular stress on:-

> a) meeting customer needs and expectations
> b) encompassing all parts of the organisation.

14.8 Six Sigma

Six sigma literally means 3.4 defects per million. In practice it is a methodical approach to improving process quality that aims for "*zero defects*" or "*get it right first time*". It was first developed by MOTOROLA in the eighties but is now widely practiced.

14.9 The Cost of Quality

Kerzner distinguishes between the Cost of Conformance and Cost of Non-conformance as follows.

14.9.1   Costs of conformance (proactive) e.g

- ➢ Training
- ➢ Indoctrination
- ➢ Verification
- ➢ Validation
- ➢ Testing
- ➢ Audits
- ➢ Maintenance
- ➢ Calibration

14.9.2   Cost of non-conformance (failure) e.g

➤ Scrap
➤ Rework
➤ Warranty repairs
➤ Complaint handling
➤ Product recalls
➤ Lost future business

The cost of non-conformance will always exceed the cost of conformance which leads to the assertion by Philip Crosby that "Quality is Free". Deming says that at least 85 percent of the costs of poor quality are the direct responsibility of management.

14.10   Benchmarking

Most major companies aspire to become "*World Class*" or "*Best in Class*". To do this it is necessary to compare practices and products with those of other companies in order to set **Benchmarks** to measure yourself against. Use of various maturity models such as the Project Management Maturity Model, (see Fig. 1.3 page 21) also allow benchmarking between organisations.

14.11   Project Management Responsibilities

To finish off it must be stressed that the Project Manager carries overall responsibility for the quality of the project and the project deliverables.

The Project Manager should:

- Make sure that all project personnel are aware of the need for quality and the required quality standards and that they have received the necessary training and are capable of carrying out the work to the appropriate standard

- Make sure that there is an approved quality plan detailing all the required quality assurance and control procedures and standards and that all the project team and relevant stakeholders are familiar with the requirements of the plan.

- Make sure everyone is aware, by means of appropriate training and communication, of their roles & responsibilities for carrying out quality management actions. If necessary appoint a Quality Manager.

- Carry out monitoring and controlling actions to make sure that the product quality is being adhered to as per the quality plan, and that the outcomes of quality audits are noted and acted upon.

- Ensure there is an effective change control process in place and communicate regularly throughout the project with client and stakeholders to ensure that the project deliverables continue to be aligned with client requirements.

15 Change Control & Configuration Management

Learning Objectives

• Understand the reasons for requiring Change Control on projects

•Describe a change control process

•Understand the meaning of Configuration Management

•Describe a configuration management process and its links to change control

APMP syllabus topics 3.5, 4.7

15.1 Definition of a Change

In a projects context a change is defined as when an event occurs that requires or causes a change to be made to the Project Baseline Plan in terms of scope, cost, time or quality.

Change Control is the process by which all changes are identified and evaluated and then a decision made on whether they are approved, rejected or deferred

Changes can arise from 3 main areas:-

> ➢ From errors, omissions in the original planning.
> ➢ From evolution of project requirements or new techniques
> ➢ Legal/mandatory changes

Changes are sometimes referred to as Variations

15.2 Why Change Control is Important

"Scope Creep", where project scope keeps increasing over time; and uncontrolled change are major causes of project failure. Changes to the project baseline must be evaluated and planned with the same thoroughness as the original plan.

Scope Creep can:-

> ➢ Increase project cost
> ➢ Cause delays
> ➢ Be detrimental to quality
> ➢ Reduce morale and productivity

However we cannot prohibit project change, because change is usually beneficial, and in fact many projects would fail if no changes were allowed. In certain circumstances a change freeze may be appropriate but when changes are allowed they MUST be controlled.

Excessive change requests are usually a symptom of poor planning and requirements definition. Proper planning and consultation with all appropriate stakeholders will help minimise change requests.

15.3 The Change Control Process

1. The request is entered into the change control system. Change requests must be made in writing in the appropriate standard form.
2. An Owner is assigned to manage the change control process. (Not the change itself)
3. A brief preliminary evaluation is carried to see if it is worth further investigation and to prioritise it.
4. If the answer to the above is yes then an impact analysis is carried out.

5. CCB[*] Approve, reject or postpone the change request
6. If approved, plans, documentation, timescale and budgets etc are updated.
7. The Change Log is updated
8. All who are impacted are advised of the changes.

This process is illustrated below

Note:- CCB means Change Control Board. This is the ideal scenario but when a formal CCB does not exist, decisions will be made by the Client/Sponsor or appropriate Stakeholders or by the PM. Responsibility for minor changes may be delegated but must still go through the same formal process.

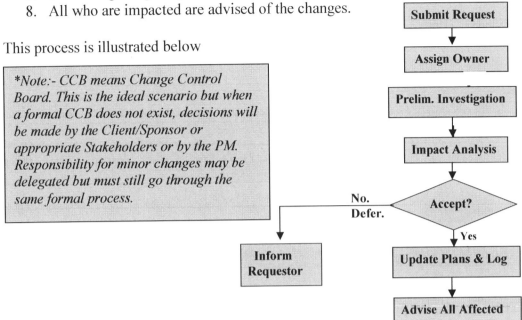

Figure 15.1 Change Control Process

All changes must be authorised so if unauthorised changes are discovered they must be retrospectively be put through the change control process. This may mean undoing some changes.

15.3.1 The Change Request Form

Changes must be formally requested on the appropriate form. Typical contents of a form are shown in figure 16.2 below.

Figure 15.2
Change Request Form

PROJECT:	Number Revision Requestor Date
ITEMS AFFECTED	Work Package Nos.
DESCRIPTION OF CHANGE	
REASON FOR CHANGE	
COST & SCHEDULE IMPACT	
EFFECT ON BUSINES CASE	
CONSQUENCE OF NOT DOING CHANGE	
ANY OTHER COMMENTS	
CHANGE APPROVED/REJECTED/REFERRED BACK	
SIGNATURES DATE	

15.3.2   Impact Assessment

Impact assessment must be carried out by people who are competent to fully understand the implications of the change on the current baseline plan. They must determine:-

- What would have to change?
- What effort would the change need?
- What is the affect on schedule / budget?
- What are the knock on effects?
- Would the business case alter?
- Would the risks increase or decrease?
- Would the agreed time for delivery change?
- Is the change within agreed tolerances?

Note: That for proposed major changes, the effort involved in analysing the impact can itself have a significant impact on the project and therefore the analysis may need to be formally approved.

15.3.3   The Change Control Log

The Change Control Log consists of the original Change Request form plus a statement of the current status and the ultimate outcome in terms of effect on schedule and budget and any other knock on effects.

The Change Control Log is an important part of the project audit trail. The Baseline Project Plan plus the Change Control Log represent the current state of the project.

Changes to the project will often result in changes to the project configuration so change control is intrinsically linked to configuration management.

15.4 Configuration Management

A product, whether it is a physical thing such as a motor car or something ethereal such as software is made up of many inter-related components. These include documents such as specifications, designs and plans as well as deliverable components. The totality of items is known as the Configuration. Configuration Management encompasses all the activities concerned with the creation, maintenance and change control of the configuration.

As a product is developed it will undergo additions and changes. Changes to one configuration item may impact others. We therefore need to control and manage these knock on effects. This is the function of a Configuration Management System.

The Configuration Management System must be totally aligned with the Change Control System. Its ability to identify possible knock on effects will facilitate change assessment and will also protect different versions of the deliverable.

Configuration Management is not just a project tool but is a key tool in the subsequent operation and maintenance of the project deliverables.

15.4.1   Configuration Management Activities

The configuration management process consists of 5 principal activities:-

1. **Configuration Management Planning**
    Establishes project specific procedures and defines tools, roles and responsibilities
2. **Configuration Identification**
    Breaking down the project deliverables into individual configuration items and creating a unique numbering system.
3. **Configuration Control**
    Maintains version control of all configuration items and the interrelationship between items.
4. **Configuration Status Accounting**
    Recording of all events that have happened to a system under development to allow comparison with the development plan and to provide traceability.
5. **Configuration Audit**
    Carried out to demonstrate that the products produced conform to the current specification and all procedures have been followed

15.4.2   Components of the Configuration Management System

The configuration management system is supported by 4 key sets of documents:-

1. **The Configuration Item Record**

    Where the item is kept, current status, dependencies on other items, cross reference to other information, change history.
    All configuration items are subject to version control

2. **The Product Description**

    A comprehensive product specification

3. **The Configuration Status Account**

    Records of all the events relating to (4) above

4. **Configuration Audit Records**

    Records of all audits carried out.

16 Budgeting, Cost Management & Earned Value

Learning Objectives

- Understand the principles and benefits of budgeting & cost management

- Understand the principles and benefits of earned value management

- Be able to perform earned value calculations and interpret earned value data

APMP syllabus topics 3.4, 3.6

16.1 The Project Budget

The budget for your project is simply the amount of money that is available to you to spend. Budgeting and Cost Management involves the estimating of project costs, the setting of a project budget and the management of the cost outcomes against that budget.

When calculating your project budget you need to include every possible cost. There are different categories of cost:-

> **Fixed Costs**
>> o 1 off non recurring costs e.g. Purchase of plant and machinery
> **Variable Costs**
>> o These rise in direct proportion to the size or duration of the project e.g. Labour, Raw Materials
> **Direct Costs**
>> o These are those costs which can be directly attributed to the project e.g. all of the above. These costs would not be incurred if the project did not exist.
> **Indirect Costs**
>> o These costs are part of the owning organisations overheads and are shared across projects/functions e.g. cost of buildings, management overheads. If the project did not exist these costs would still have to be born by the Organisation.

The relationship between the project budget and the cost categories is achieved by means of the Cost Breakdown Structure (See paragraph 10.5)
Cost estimate should also include an allowance for risk and contingency.

16.1.1   Budget Approvals

The project budget is calculated by the PM based on cost estimates. It is then approved by a project Board or Sponsor who then delegate control to the Project Manger, normally a Phase/Stage at a time. The budget is then allocated to Team Leaders and then to the project team according to the Work Breakdown Structure
Budgets are controlled at Task level and rolled up for reporting purposes as per the Cost Breakdown Structure. Deviations from the budget are managed with appropriate escalation levels.

16.1.2   The Cost Budgeting Process

Cost budgeting involves aggregating the estimated costs of all work packages over time to establish a total cost baseline for measuring project progress. Consider the Gantt chart shown opposite which shows the allocation and aggregation of resources at task level.

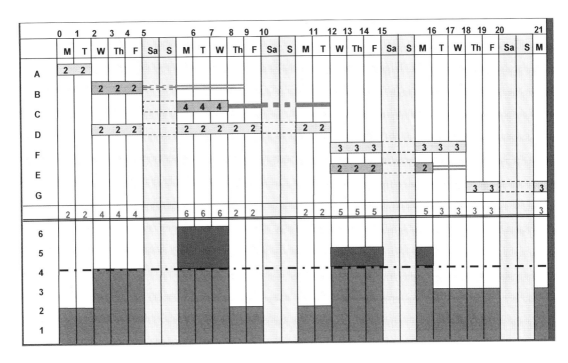

Figure 16.1 Resource Gantt Chart

Imagine each resource above cost £500/day. Then we can show the daily costs as follows and then calculate the cumulative cost curve and plot it as shown

Week	1	2	3	4	5	6	7	8	9	10	11	12	13	14	15	16	17	18	19	20	21
Resource	2	2	4	4	4	6	6	6	2	2	2	2	5	5	5	5	3	3	3	3	3
Cost £K	10	10	20	20	20	30	30	30	10	10	10	10	25	25	25	25	15	15	15	15	15
Cum Cost	10	20	40	60	80	110	140	170	180	190	200	210	235	260	285	310	325	340	355	370	385

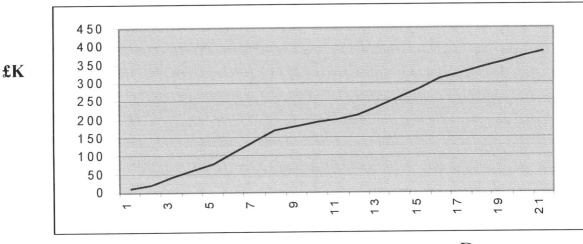

Figure 16.2 Budget Curve (S-Curve)

Days

This is the S (for Summation) curve or Budget curve that provides us with us a budget baseline against which we can monitor progress. This is the foundation of Earned Value which we will discuss later in this section.

16.1.3 Cash Flow

Cash Flow concerns the planning of project spending relative to income in such a way as to minimize the carrying cost of the financing for the project. For any project (or organisation) it is important to forecast and manage cash flow so as to ensure cash is available when needed. Companies manage cash flow by getting in debt as quickly as possible and by paying bills as late as possible.

Cost Accruals are for things that have been purchased but payment has not been made. Delaying payment improves cash flow.

Revenues can also be accrued.
   Sales are recognised (i.e. counted towards profit) when they are made, rather than when cash is received

Cash Flow is not the same as Profit/Loss. Companies trading at a profit can still go bust because of negative cash flow and vice versa.

16.1.4 Cost Commitment

The graph below illustrates that for any project, moral and practical commitments are made ahead of binding legal commitments and that actual spend i.e. Cash Flow, lags behind. Costs that have been committed to are referred to as Sunk Costs. Sunk costs will still be incurred even if the project is terminated.

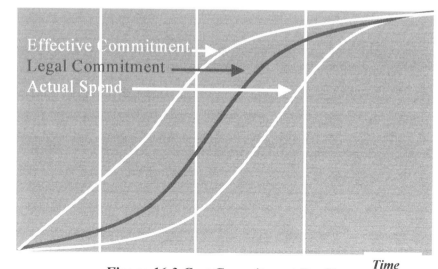

Figure 16.3 Cost Commitment Profile

16.1.5   Cost reporting

It is the responsibility of the PM to see that all project costs are monitored.
The following need to be reported on a routine basis:-

- ➢ Variances from the budget at task and project level and reasons for variance

- ➢ Budget adjustments due to formal changes

- ➢ Cash flow forecast

- ➢ Cash in, cash out

- ➢ Revenues and costs recognised

- ➢ Project cost/margin forecast

16.2 Earned Value

The principles of Earned Value will be
demonstrated using a simple example.

You have just employed a bricklayer to build
a wall. The wall in question contains 1,000
bricks which the bricklayer estimates will
cost 50p each. He is going to charge you £ 50
per day for the estimated 10 days of work. So
the total planned cost of the wall is £1,000.

•In Earned Value Management terms this
expected cost is the **Planned Cost – PC**
(This is the S-curve)

•You have planned to pay for the wall in two instalments of £500. One after 5 days and the
other on completion in 10 day's time.

•After five days you receive a bill for £ 375. This is the **Actual Cost-AC**

•Is this good news or bad news? Let us see what the graph overleaf tells us about the status of
the project?

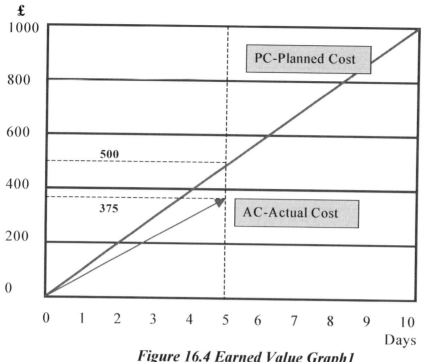

Figure 16.4 Earned Value Graph1

This graph tells us what we have spent and what we should have spent. *It says nothing about what we have achieved.*

You decide to visit the wall. To your horror you find that only 250 bricks have been laid. Based on the original estimate of £ 1,000 for a wall of 1,000 bricks, the "value" of each brick laid is £ 1.

The value of the work done so far is therefore only £ 250. This is the Earned Value. The situation is illustrated in figure 16.5 opposite.

Not only have you paid £375 for what you thought was going to cost £250, but only a quarter of the wall has been finished when it should have been a half.

Let's quantify what's happened.

We can calculate **Schedule Variance (SV)**

   SV = Earned Value (EV) – Planned Value (PV)   =   250-500 = -250

We can also calculate **Cost Variance (CV)**

   CV = Earned Value (EV) - Actual cost (AC)   =   250-375 = -125

Both are negative, indicating that the project is behind schedule and over budget.

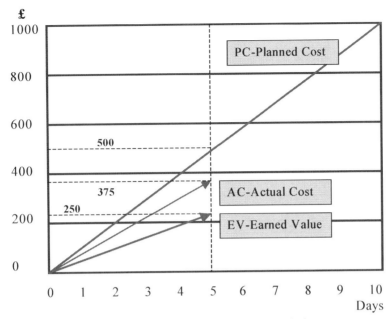

Figure 16.5 Earned Value Graph 2

16.2.1   Performance Indices

We can calculate cost and performance ratios to indicate project performance.

Cost Performance Index (CPI) (efficiency)   = EV/AC

Schedule Performance Index (SPI)   = EV/PC

Values less than 1 indicate a project is over budget and late.
Values more than1 indicate under budget and early.

16.2.2   Forecasting

We can use the Earned Value information to forecast the final project outcome at any point in the project.

16.2.2.1   Forecasting Cost

Budget at Completion (BAC) is the project budget or "Total Planned Cost"

There are two different assumptions used to calculate Estimate Cost at Completion (EAC)

Assumption 1 assumes everything will be on plan from now on. We apply the formula:-

$$EAC = BAC - CV$$

In other words the current Cost Variance will be maintained until the end of the project.

Assumption 2 assumes that the remainder of the project will carry on with the same average efficiency so far.

$$EAC = BAC/CPI$$

16.2.2.2   Forecasting Time

This is not as straightforward as forecasting money.

Assumption 1. Estimated Completion Date (ECD) = Current Planned Date + Slippage

Again this assumes that future work will be on plan but how do we calculate slippage in terms of time? SV (Schedule Variance) is measured in money. The answer is that we use the earned value graph to convert money to time as shown below.

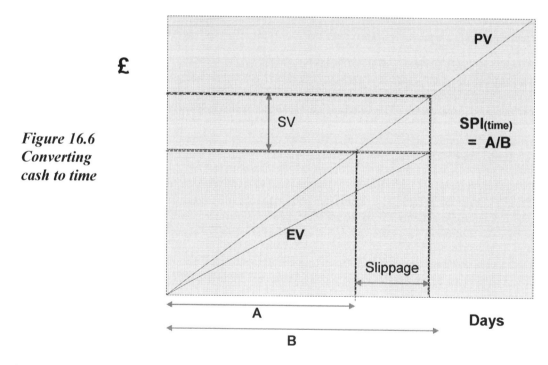

*Figure 16.6
Converting
cash to time*

Assumption 2. Estimated Completion Date = Original Duration/SPI

This assumes once again that all remaining work will have the same SPI.
Unfortunately this method will give wrong results if the planned end date has already been exceeded. This is because at the end of a project Earned Value approaches Planned Value and

thus SPI approaches 1 regardless of performance. (The Earned Value can never exceed the Planned Value because once EV reaches PC then the work is complete)

It is valid to use SPI to forecast the revised end date right up to the planned end date. However once this date has been passed another method must be used.

We calculate a new SPI called SPI(time) = A/B in figure 16.6

Then Estimated Completion Date = Original Duration/ SPI(time)

This method is valid over the entire range of the project, both before and after the planned end date and so is the preferred method.

16.2.3   Requirements for Earned Value

In order for Earned Value to work the following elements need to be in place.

> A Work Breakdown Structure
> Assigned responsibilities for each task.
> Allocation of direct cost budget via the WBS
> All tasks scheduled
> A method of measuring achievement for each task
> Cost and achievement data collected at regular planned intervals
> A time phased budget baseline plan
> Baseline changes managed through change control

Note that non productive activities such as management overheads, i.e. tasks that do not directly add value, are not normally included in EV calculations. Nor are major one off purchases such as capital equipment.

16.2.4   Earned Value Pros & Cons

Pros

> Focuses on useful work done not just on money/time spent
> Measures the whole project rather than concentrating on the Critical Path
> Allows us to forecast the project outcome using different assumptions
> Allows us to easily plot and monitor trends
> The requirement to measure real %age complete demands tighter control

Cons

- ➤ Because the technique takes a whole view, over-performance in 1 area may hide under-performance in another
- ➤ Slippage forecast based on SV or SPI will only give the same result as the schedule if all slippage is on the critical path
- ➤ Slippage forecasts take the average slope of the EV line up to the current time so take no account of any recent change in the trend.
- ➤ It requires considerable administrative organisation & effort

17 Communications & Information Management

Learning Objectives

• Understand the meaning of Information Management

• Project reporting requirements

• Understand the importance of effective project communications

• The Communications Management Plan

• Describe barriers to communication and how they maybe overcome

APMP syllabus topics 3.7, 7.1

17.1 Information Management definition

Information management is concerned with the organisation and control of project information. It is important that the project has an effective information management system which can take in appropriate information and formally report that information to stakeholders.

The System should encompass:-
- ➤ **Collection**
    - o How project information is to be acquired i.e. source and medium
- ➤ **Storage**
    - o How the information is to be stored including medium, access control and version control
- ➤ **Dissemination**
    - o How information is distributed to stakeholders
- ➤ **Archiving**
    - o The procedures for archiving inactive information whilst keeping it accessible
- ➤ **Destruction**
    - o Procedures for defining when and how archive data can be legally destroyed

17.2 Document Management

Document Management is a key component of Information Management. The minimum requirements for such a system are:-
- ➤ It should cater for every document and record* type e.g. book, drawing, report, letters, minutes, specifications etc
- ➤ It should list all documents and state where they are stored and the media type
- ➤ It should maintain version control
- ➤ It should facilitate easy retrieval
- ➤ It should support access controls

*Documents means the entirety of project documentation.
 Records usually refers to policy and regulatory items.

17.3 Project Reporting

It is the responsibility of the PM to ensure that all relevant project information is communicated to the Sponsor and appropriate stakeholders in a timely and effective manner. There will be ongoing informal communication at all times but project status should be formally reported, usually on a monthly basis and at key points such as phase ends. To do this the PM will require formal reports from appropriate team members which must then be collated and simplified for passage upwards. It should be stressed that formal reporting is not a substitute for ongoing project communication. Information must be presented in a timely fashion and it may not be appropriate to wait until the next monthly report. Avoid overloading Stakeholders with too much information and use Exception Reporting when appropriate.

17.3.1   Report Structure

A project status report should be clear and concise with a consistent structure and layout such as the following.

1. A short management summary containing key information. Some stakeholders will not read beyond this.
2. List achievements and progress since last status update was given
3. List delays and problems since last status update was given
    - List corrective actions being taken
    - Address schedule implications
4. Outline Plan for next period
    - Planned deliverables
    - Milestones
    - Potential problems
    - Help required
5. Earned Value Report
    - Earned Value Graph
    - Cost & Schedule Variances
    - Cost & Schedule Completion Forecasts

17.4 Communications Management

Communications Management is concerned all the ways in which information is exchanged and interpreted. This is achieved in 3 main ways, written, verbal and by body language.

17.4.1   Written

Written communication is permanent. It is memory independent but can still be ambiguous and open to interpretation

E-mail, although written, has some of the elements of speech because it is immediate and it is easy to send something you may have cause to regret. However unlike speech or ordinary written communications it can literally be published to the world in minutes

17.4.2   Verbal

The majority of our communication is done this way. The advantage is that it is fast, easy and natural. However spoken words are transient and are easily misunderstood and may be recalled in different ways

17.4.3   Body Language

Body language can give away our feelings even when they contradict our words and can convey a message without using words.

17.5 *Channels of Communication*

Most of what a project manager does involves communication and there are innumerable channels of communication available, many of which make increasing use of technology.

17.5.1.1   Examples

➢ Meetings	➢ Blogs
➢ Presentations	➢ e-mails
➢ Telephone	➢ Progress Reports
➢ One to one	➢ Fax
➢ Video Conferencing	➢ Letters
➢ Text messaging	➢ Drawings
➢ Newsletters	➢ Specifications
➢ Contracts	➢ Internet
➢ Websites	➢ Publications

17.6 *Barriers to Communication*

There are many things that can get in the way of the transmission and reception of a message. The following are examples of these barriers to communication.

17.6.1   Environmental Barriers

These are barriers that arise from the environment in which the communication is taking place. e.g

➢ Noise distractions
➢ Too high or low temperature
➢ Poor air quality
➢ Visual distractions
➢ The medium
➢ Information overload

17.6.2   Background

We filter the words of others based upon our technical, social and educational background e.g.

➢ Jargon
➢ Culture

- Language
- Social class
- Financial status

17.6.3   Personal

This involves things personal to ourselves. e.g.

- Tiredness
- Hunger
- Thirst
- Personal prejudice
- Preconceptions
- Stereotyping
- Culture

17.6.4   Organisational

This is to do with factors within your organisation .e.g

- Relative seniority
- Security
- Company culture

17.7 Effective Communications

The ability to communicate is probably the most important skill a project manager possesses. The following factors will greatly enhance the effectiveness of communications.

- Always use the most appropriate means to communicate
- Ask for and give feedback
- Be aware of blockers and barriers
- Do not be a communications bottleneck
- Use standard reporting formats
- Use exception reporting
- Keep all stakeholders aware of important events/changes
- Restrict meetings to appropriate personnel
- Have a Communications Management Plan
- Hold effective meetings (see 17.7.2)

17.7.1   The Communications Management Plan

On any project informal communication will arise naturally. However much of the required communication is formal and should be properly planned and documented in a Communications Management Plan. This plan should do the following:-

- Detail and describe all the project information requirements
- Detail means of acquiring information
- Describe the methods by which information will be stored
- Describe how information will be secured and access to it controlled
- Describe a distribution system that details to whom information will flow including format, content and level of detail
- Establish the project reporting structure
- Provide schedules showing when each type of communication will be produced and to whom it is sent (see example of Communications Matrix below)
- Describe methods for updating information

Key W - Weekly M - Monthly Q - Quarterly A - As required	Sponsor/ Board	Client Manager	Programme Manager	Project Manager	Functional Managers	Project Office	Manager User	Representative	Team Leaders	Project Team
Project Plan										
Change Log										
Risk register										
Project Status										
Project Schedule										
Milestone report										
Etc etc										

Figure 17.1 Communications Matrix

17.7.2   Effective Meetings

There are probably more man hours lost through ineffective meetings than any other cause. The application of some simple rules can make meetings much more effective.

- Have a meeting policy defined in the Communications Plan
- Meet only when there is a need to meet and not just because it is a routine
- Circulate an agenda before the meeting and stick to it

- Encourage participation and do not invite non participants
- Include team building wherever possible
- Issue minutes as soon as possible after the meeting
- Make all actions personal and timely and follow them up
- Only attend meetings you can contribute to or benefit from
- Prepare your personal contribution to the meeting

Remember poor meetings result from poor preparation and a poor chairman.

18 Procurement & Negotiation

Learning Objectives

• Describe the process of Supplier selection

• Explain Procurement strategy

• Describe the different types of supplier contracts/reimbursement

• Distinguish between different contractual relationships

• Understand the process of Negotiation

APMP syllabus topics 5.4, 7.5

18.1 Definitions

Procurement
The securing (or acquisition) of goods or services.

Procurement (or Acquisition) Strategy
Determining the most appropriate means of procuring the component parts or services of a project

Contract
An agreement between two parties which is legally binding'

Contractor
A person, company or firm who holds a contract for carrying out the works and/or the supply of goods in connection with the Project

Supplier
Any organization, including contractors and consultants, that supply goods or services to customers.

18.2 The Procurement Process

The overall procurement process is illustrated in the flowchart below.

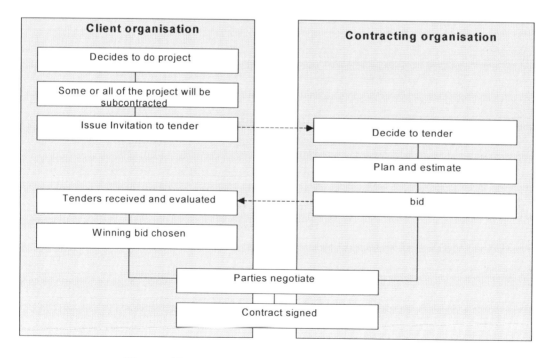

Figure 18.1 The Procurement Process

18.3 Procurement Strategy

Before an organisation issues an "Invitation to Tender" (ITT) it needs to consider a number of strategic issues that will affect the nature of the eventual contract. e.g.

> ➤ The initial make-or-buy decision based on a comparison of the actual costs and benefits of both options (see 18.4)
> ➤ What form of contract will be used? (see 18.5)
> ➤ How suppliers will be selected (see 18.7)
> ➤ The kind of relationship required (see 18.8)
> ➤ Whether to use a single supplier or multiple suppliers
> ➤ What will be the payment terms and pricing structure?

The answers to these questions will go a long way towards determining the most appropriate contract type.

18.4 Make or Buy

Make or buy analysis should include the following factors.

1. The direct costs of a prospective procurement.

2. The indirect costs – i.e. the cost of managing and monitoring the purchasing process

3. The overall effect of the decision on the organisation e.g. would a decision to **Make** have a knock on effect on other projects which may require the *same* resources. Would a decision to buy put in house facilities at risk?

18.5 Main Types of Contract

Although there are many variations we will cover here the four main types of contract.

1. Cost Plus Percentage of Cost
    a. Cost reimbursable
    b. Time and Materials
2. Cost Plus Fixed Fee
3. Cost Plus Incentive Fee
4. Firm Fixed Price

18.5.1   Cost Plus Percentage of Cost

There are two classes of cost plus contracts:

a) Cost reimbursable

In this type of contract the Seller is reimbursed for all costs, both direct and indirect with an agree percentage mark up on the cost as profit. The agreed upon percentage infers an "open book" approach. This means that the buyer has unrestricted access to the seller's accounts to determine the actual costs incurred. This is called "open book"

The Seller is obligated only to make best effort to fulfil the contract within the estimated amount. If the seller fails to do this the buyer funds all overruns. Thus the seller cannot make a loss and the buyer carries all the risk. In cost reimbursable contracts the work is usually carried out on the supplier premises and the buyer has little control.

b) Time and Materials (T&M)

As before the seller is reimbursed for all costs plus a percentage mark up. The difference to the previous scenario is that it is not "open book". The supplier's profit margin is unknown to the buyer. Another difference is that in T&M the Contractor usually just supplies labour and sometimes materials, and the Client often supervises the work. Thus T&M is less risky for the client because of the closer control although in both these contract types there is no incentive for the seller to control costs.

18.5.2   Cost Plus Fixed Fee

Here contract costs are reimbursed as before but instead of adding a percentage mark up there is a fixed fee that is paid in instalments as the contract progresses
The ceiling on the seller's profit means that there is some motivation to control costs, but most risk remains with the buyer. However this can be an unsatisfactory contract for the seller as an overrun will reduce the margin percentage even though the £ margin is fixed. These contracts can be open or closed book.

18.5.3   Cost Plus Incentive Fee (Target Cost)

Contract costs are reimbursed as before but as well as a percentage mark up there is an incentive fee that is linked to a target. If the project comes in on target the incentive fee is paid. As a variation the incentive fee may vary depending on over or underachievement of the target according to an agreed formulae. There is now an incentive on the seller to control costs, so that risk for the buyer is reduced/shared

This approach can be used when entering into partnerships or alliances and the approach is one of shared risk and reward. It can also be a compromise when the supplier is unwilling to take all the risk with a fixed price and the client is unwilling to take on the risk of cost reimbursement.

18.5.4   Firm Fixed Price (FFP)

With a FFP contract the seller furnishes goods or services at a fixed price regardless as to how much it cost to provide them. Thus the seller bears all the risk. For such contracts the seller will normally build in cost contingencies and include a risk premium.

If risks are well controlled there is a greater profit potential than for cost reimbursable projects. This approach is best suited for situations were the specifications are well defined and costs are predictable. For less predictable situations a wise seller will increase his risk premium or insist on cost reimbursable.

Sometimes contractors negotiate to be allowed to pass on cost increases for labour and raw materials. This puts some of the risk back on the client. This might then be called Fixed Price rather than Firm Fixed Price.

18.6 Contract Payment Structures

The two extremes of payment structures are Fixed Price and Cost Reimbursable where the largest share of the risk lies with the Seller and Buyer respectively. Having a Target Cost is one way to help share risk but there are two further payment structures that can reduce risk to the supplier in a fixed price situation.

18.6.1   Milestone Payments

This approach is most suitable when a contract can be split into defined stages and/or where stage definition depends on earlier stages. It can also be used when a client does not wish to commit to everything up front. At each stage something of value is supplied and this can be evaluated before committing further funds. The Supplier has on incentive to achieve at each stage, in order to receive further work, and cash flow is improved. Total risk to the Supplier is reduced and variations contained within stages

18.6.2   Unit Rate Based Payment

This is similar to previous example except pieces of work are very much smaller. It is suitable when the work to be done, or resources required is uncertain at the time of the bid and the client would rather "pay as you go" The supplier has an incentive to achieve at each unit of work and cash flow is much more favourable as payment is made for each piece of work. As the contract is still fixed price the risk is still with the Supplier but less than for the previous examples as the work is in much smaller packages.

18.7 Supplier Selection Criteria

Picking good suppliers is of critical importance. They are much harder to control than your internal resources and a poor supplier or sub-contractor can do immense harm to your project. To become an approved supplier to your project or organisation suppliers must be qualified. We can apply some selection criteria early in the process i.e. the **pre-qualification** stage which looks at things such as:-

> ➢ Financial status
> ➢ Industry knowledge

- Delivery capability
- Quality System
- Relevant experience
- Quality of previous work

During the **tendering** process we can look at fewer suppliers in more depth, asking questions such as:-

- Likely working relationship
- Depth of planning in tender document
- Are costs and schedule realistic and competitive
- Product life cycle costs
- Are expectations of client and contractor in harmony?
- Contract type e.g Fixed Price, T&M, mixed
- Quality of Project Management

18.7.1   Supplier Evaluation Tool

A weighting system (opposite) for attaching relative importance to the evaluation criteria will make selection more objective and less subject to personal prejudice.

	Score 1-5	Weight 1-5	Total
Life Cycle Costs	5	5	25
Seller Capability	1	4	4
Financial Status of Seller	3	3	9
Seller Track record	1	3	3
Seller Industry Knowledge	1	2	2
Delivery Capability	5	5	25
Quality System	2	2	4
Project Management	5	4	20
		Total	92

Figure 18.2 Supplier weighting system

Such a method will also help to demonstrate that the selection process has been fair.

18.7.2   Bidders Conference

It is a mandatory requirement that the tendering process must be seen to be open and fair to all potential bidders. This requires that all bidders must be given exactly the same information on which to base their bid. Information given to one must be given to all. Even with well prepared bid documents there will be ambiguities and differences in interpretation. Any such problems can be addressed at a Bidders Conference where all potential suppliers can attend and ask questions. If this is impractical the conference could be web based.

18.8 Contractual Relationships

There are many ways in which parties can contract with each other. Some of the more common relationships are as follows:-

18.8.1   Arms Length

This is the traditional buyer/seller relationship where there is minimal contact between the parties. Transactions are often one off or irregular.

18.8.2   Preferred Supplier

This is a much closer, longer term relationship. The seller will typically appoint an account manager to manage the relationship and grow the business. It is often used for security of supply of key goods.

18.8.3   Partnering/Alliancing/Joint Venture

This involves a long-term commitment between two or more organisations in achieving common objectives. It can vary from an agreement to collaborate on a single project right up to forming a new joint venture company to develop and launch a new product or facility.

18.8.4   Turnkey

This is where a Supplier undertakes to provide a total solution for which the Buyer can literally take delivery and "turn the key" to switch it on.

18.9 Negotiation

An ability to negotiate successfully is a key project management skill.
Negotiation will take place with:-

- Contractors & Suppliers
- End Users
- Resource Providers
- Team Members
- Project Sponsor
- Stakeholders

Negotiations typically go through five defined stages. They are:-

1. Preparation
2. Discussion
3. Proposition
4. Bargaining
5. Agreement

18.9.1   Preparation

This is the most important stage of all. You should:

➢ List all the points to be negotiated and your preferred order of dealing with them
➢ Establish and rank your objectives
  o   What you would like to get
  o   What would you reasonably settle for
  o   What you must get otherwise you walk away
  o   What concessions are you prepared to make
➢ Gather, review and digest all available information-Knowledge is power
➢ Evaluate your strengths and weaknesses (sources of power, see below) and that of your "opponent"

➢ Rehearse the negotiation and prepare responses to difficult questions
➢ Decide on your negotiating team and who will lead it.

The difference between each parties "walk away point" defines the "scope for bargaining" as shown below.

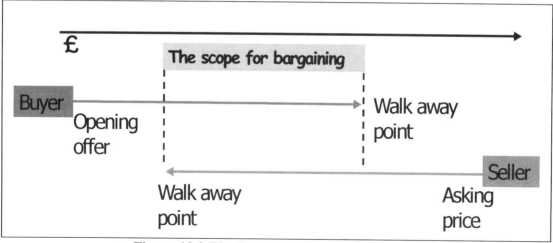

Figure 18.3 The Scope for Bargaining

Most agreements tend to fall somewhere in the middle of the range of the first positions signalled. Thus great care is needed in positioning the initial bid. Each negotiator will strive to push the other as near as possible to his walk away point.

18.9.2   Discussion

This is the first face to face stage where the intention is to establish rapport, clarify purpose and agenda, check information and generally form a firm base on which to negotiate.

18.9.3   Proposition

The Seller will normally state his opening offer or the proposal may be known in which case the buyer may make a counter offer. This then establishes the difference between the two positions and marks the start of the bargaining process.

18.9.4   Bargaining

This can often be a lengthy process. There are many tactics that are employed in the bargaining process (see below). There are however a few basic rules to be obeyed.

1. To gain agreement, try to link issues e.g if you do this then maybe we could do that.
2. Do not give something for nothing. Do not make a concession without getting something in return.
3. Be aware of tactics such as:-

   - **Price**
     - o Buyers will always say your price is too high
   - **Deadline**
     - o If you apply deadlines for agreement   then be sure you mean it.
   - **Fait Accompli**
     - o Something already decided on which you refuse to compromise
   - **Limited Authority**
     - o The person agreeing the deal has to go and get approval of his management. Approval is then refused and you restart negotiation from a new base.
   - **Foggy Memory**
     - o Denial of something previously agreed but not documented.
   - **Fair & Reasonable**
     - o Claiming that your terms are fair and reasonable and should be agreed to.
   - **Extreme demands**
     - o Make an extreme opening offer then appearing to make concessions to get the price you always had in mind.
   - **Good Guy/bad Guy**
     - o The "bad guy" makes extreme demands then the "good guy" modifies them
   - **Control**
     - o Establishing who is in charge by for instance making the other parties wait before seeing them.
   - **Violins**
     - o Pleading lack of money.
   - **Surprise**
     - o Deliberately bringing up a completely new point

- ➤ **Budget Limit**
  - ○ We don't have a sufficient budget to meet your price.
- ➤ **Future Carrot**
  - ○ The promise of future business if you reduce prices for this negotiation.
- ➤ **Ultimatum**
  - ○ Take it or leave. (A risky practice if you are bluffing)
- ➤ **Broken Record**
  - ○ Repeating the same demands and refusing to move.
- ➤ **Silence**
  - ○ Simply say nothing and wait for your opponent to "crack". Can be embarrassing when both parties use it at the same time.

18.9.5   Agreement

Review and document what has been agreed. Even if you are not formally signing the final contract at that time you must document and sign the agreement reached so there is no possibility of misunderstanding or later retractment.

18.10   *Sources of Power in Negotiation*

In a negotiation both sides have power. The side with the most "power" will generally get the best deal.

- ➤ Need
  - ○ Who needs agreement most? The salesman who is desperate for the order to make his numbers is in a weak position.
- ➤ Insight
  - ○ Who has most "inside information"? Knowing about your opponents weaknesses and problems can be a source of power
- ➤ Options
  - ○ Who has other options? If you are the only supplier who can deliver on time then you have a position of power.
- ➤ Negotiation Skill
  - ○ Who is the better negotiator? Skill is power.
- ➤ Investment
  - ○ How much previous time/money been invested? A salesman will find it hard to walk away from a deal that has been months in the making
- ➤ Planning & Preparation
  - ○ Who has prepared better? This is where we started from. Planning and preparation is the key to a successful negotiation.

19 Teamwork

Learning Objectives

•Differentiate between groups and teams

•Understand how teams develop

•Describe the features of a high performance team

•Understand the Belbin model of team dynamics

APMP syllabus topics 7.2

19.1 Teams & Groups

19.1.1 A Team Definition

".. two or more people who interact, dynamically, interdependently, and adaptively toward a common and valued goal/objective/ mission, who have each been assigned specific roles or functions to perform"

Salas, Dickenson, Converse and Tannenbaum

Project teams are normally transient and will be disbanded upon completion of the project.

A **Group** is not the same as a team

> - The people in a group have no common objective or vision
> - They do not have specific assigned roles
> - They are not interdependent
> - They do not exhibit the characteristics of a team

19.1.2 Working Groups

A working group is a hybrid between a team and a group. In a working group work is allocated to individuals who work alone and the leader does the coordinating.

19.1.3 Characteristics of Effective Teams

> - They have a good leader
> - There is a good blend of skills and personalities
> - Team morale and motivation is high
> - The team works together and everyone participates actively and positively in meetings and activities
> - Everyone knows their own role in the team
> - Team goals are given realistic time frames.
> - Everyone is focused on the ultimate goal of the project
> - Team goals are understood by everyone.
> - Everyone is supportive of the project and of others
> - There is trust between team members

19.2 Belbin Roles

Dr. Raymond Meredith Belbin carried out research in the sixties on how people work within teams. He concluded that their were eight role types within a team and that team work better if all of those roles are represented in the team. This does not mean that a team must have 8 people because most people can adopt more than one role even though one one role is often strongest.

Certain roles work well together and others not so well. There is a simple written test which purports to tell which roles a person is best suited for. This is useful information for a project manager. However with experience and knowledge of the role types it is possible to accurately determine role types without the test.

Belbin later added a ninth role, that of specialist brought in purely for their expert knowledge in a particular area.

The roles are illustrated below.

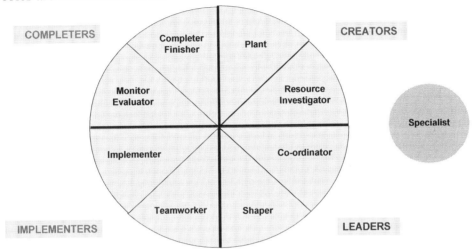

Figure 19.1 Belbin Roles

The roles are briefly described in the table below along with their weaknesses

Team Role	Description	Allowable Weaknesses	Not Allowable
Coordinator	Mature, confident, clarifies goals	Manipulative, lazy (own work)	Take credit for teams work
Shaper	Challenging, full of drive dynamic	Provokes others, hurts feelings	No apologies, no humour
Monitor Evaluator	Sober, strategic, sees options	Lacks drive, overly critical	Cynicism without logic
Team worker	Cooperative, mild, diplomatic	Indecisive, easily influenced	Avoiding pressure situations
Plant	Creative, unorthodox	Ignores details, preoccupied	Ownership vs. cooperation
Implementer	Disciplined, reliable, practical	Inflexible, slow to respond	Obstructing change
Completer / finisher	Painstaking, conscientious	Inclined to worry, nit-picker	Obsessive behaviour
Resource investigator	Develop contacts, enthusiastic	Overoptimistic, loses interest	Letting clients down
Specialist	Single minded, rare knowledge	Overlooks big picture	Ignoring important info.

19.3 Team Building

When teams work together, and support each other, the team is much more than the sum of its parts. The team consists of a diverse collection of individuals with widely differing backgrounds, abilities, needs, and interests. Team members are initially unfamiliar with project goals and individuals' capabilities are unknown to the project manager. In addition matrix management mode makes it hard to obtain real commitments from team members who may work on the project part-time and/or temporary. Team building should be very high on a project manager's priority list and be a continuous activity. It is very easy to spot a poor performing team. It will exhibit some or all of the following symptoms.

➢ Frustration
➢ Unhealthy conflict
➢ Unproductive meetings
➢ Lack of trust in the PM

The results of good team building are also very apparent.
➢ Members are ready to work to a common goal
➢ There is team loyalty and identification
➢ Members are willing to work hard for the good of the team
➢ They are willing to sacrifice personal interests for the team good
➢ Team morale is high

19.4 Stages in Team Development

The most widely used model of team development is the "Forming, Storming, Norming, Performing model". This model is illustrated below.

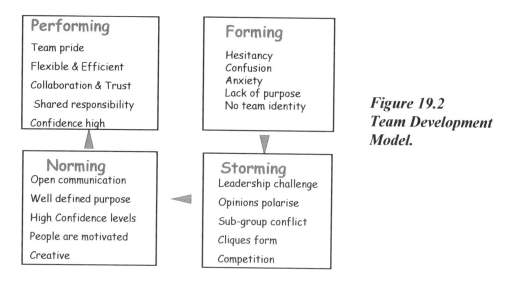

Figure 19.2
Team Development Model.

This is a well recognised process that all teams go through. The job of the PM is to get the team performing and keep them there. The PM must also realise that going through the stages from Norming to Performing is natural and must be expected, Events such as team changes, change in objectives, uncontrolled changes or setbacks can cause a team to stop performing and revert to storming.

The way in which the model relates to project activities and what must take place to progress from one stage to the next is illustrated below.

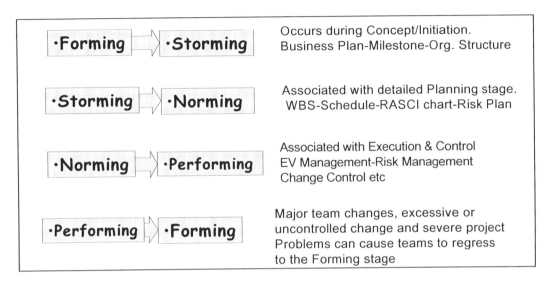

Figure 19.3 Stage Progression

19.5 Effective Team Building

Team building must be planned by the PM and become an integral part of the process of project management.

> ➢ Hold a kick off meeting.
> ➢ Make sure everyone contributes to and "buys in" to the project plan
> ➢ Make sure everyone knows exactly what is expected of them.
> ➢ Understand, support and coach each individual
> ➢ Hold regular team building events.
> ➢ Praise in public, reprimand in private
> ➢ Provide motivation, reward and recognition
> ➢ Provide for skills development
> ➢ Shield your team from outside interference
> ➢ Celebrate successes and commiserate setbacks...as a team

20 Leadership & Conflict Management

Learning Objectives

• Describe typical leadership qualities

• Describe a situational leadership model

• Explain the principles of motivation and standard motivational theories

• Describe sources of conflict in projects

• Explain a conflict resolution model

APMP syllabus topics 7.3, 7.4

20.1 The Project Manager as Leader

Project managers are expected to plan, manage and organise but the most important skill is Leadership. Leadership is mainly based on example and good communication skills

Good Leaders:-
> Lead by example-are Role Models
> Are good communicators, especially listening
> Are seen to be fair and even handed
> Are good at the other aspects of project management
> Command respect
> Care about people
> Will take risks for, and stand up for their people
> Will always be there for the team
> Know what is going on

20.1.1 Leadership Activities

20.1.1.1 Give Feedback

Even though team members may only work for you on a temporary basis and have their own line manager the PM must still provide constructive feedback to enable people to develop their skills and improve on their weak areas

20.1.1.2 Recognise Achievement

People expect hard work and achievement to be recognised. They also require a record of that recognition so do it in writing.

20.1.1.3 Reward Success

Recognition is essential but people also expect to be rewarded. Public recognition is a form of reward but eventually rewards must be tangible.

20.1.1.4 Encourage and Support

A good leader will spend time coaching and encouraging people become more effective.

20.1.1.5 Set Realistic Goals & Objectives

The setting of individual and team goals is a key activity. Goals must be challenging but not so difficult as to become de-motivating. Individual goals must be compatible and aligned with the needs of the project.

20.1.1.6 Be Available

Finally a good leader will make sure he is available to his team and maximises face to face contact. This can be difficult to achieve on geographically dispersed projects.

20.2 Leadership Styles (Hersey & Blanchard)

Hersey and Blanchard developed what they called a *Situational Leadership Model.* In simple terms, a situational leader is one who can adopt different leadership styles depending on the situation.

They defined 4 basic leadership styles for getting tasks done:-
- ➤ Directing
- ➤ Coaching
- ➤ Supporting
- ➤ Delegating

These four styles can be expressed in terms of *Supporting Behaviour* (concern for the person) and *Directive Behaviour* (concern for the task). This is illustrated below.

High	**Supporting** Leader facilitates and takes part in decisions, but day to day control is with the follower.	**Coaching** Leader defines roles and tasks of the follower and supervises closely. Communication is largely one way.
Supporting Behaviour (Concern for the Person)	**Delegating** Leader sets direction then stands back. The follower decides when and how the leader will be involved	**Directing** Leaders define roles and tasks of the 'follower', and supervise them closely. Decisions are made by the leader. Communication is largely one-way.
Low	Directive Behaviour(Concern for the Task)	**High**

Figure 20.1 Hersey Blanchard Situational Leadership Model

There is no single correct way of leading. Most leaders have a natural style of working but the most appropriate style will vary with the importance of the task and the motivation and competence of the "follower".

20.3 Motivation

"People who are unable to motivate themselves must be content with mediocrity, no matter how impressive their other talents."

Andrew Carnegie

Performance is a function of ability and motivation. It follows that a key attribute of leadership is the ability to motivate others to perform to their maximum ability.
The two most well known theories of motivation are:-
- ➢ Maslow's Hierarchy of Needs
- ➢ Hertzberg's Hygiene Theory

20.3.1   Maslow's Hierarchy of Needs

Maslow maintained that the needs of individuals form a hierarchy and that one cannot proceed to a higher level until the lower level needs are fully satisfied. This is illustrated below.

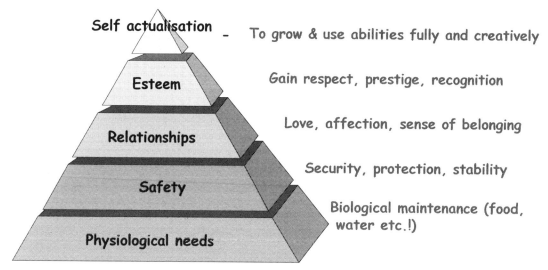

Figure 20.2 Maslow's Hierarchy of Needs

This is a generalised model and the table below shows how this relates to the working environment and organisational factors.

Needs level	General Rewards	Organisational factors
1 Physiological	Food, water, sleep	Pay Pleasant working conditions Cafeteria
2 Safety	Safety, security, stability, protection	Safe working conditions Company benefits Job security
3 Social	Friendship, affection, belongingness	Cohesive work group Friendly supervision Professional associations
4 Esteem	Self-esteem, self-respect, prestige, status	Social recognition Job title High status job
5 Self-actualisation	Growth, advancement, creativity	Challenging job Opportunities for creativity Achievement in work Advancement

20.3.2   Hertzberg's Hygiene Theory

Herzberg developed a theory of motivation based on what he describes as Hygiene Factors and Motivators.

Examples of Hygiene Factors
- Working conditions
- Salary
- Quality of management/supervision

Satisfactory hygiene factors are necessary, but not sufficient for a contented worker. Poor hygiene factors may destroy motivation; but improving hygiene factors under normal circumstances is not likely to increase motivation and if it does it is usually short term.

20.3.2.1   Examples of Motivators

- Recognition
- Work content
- Responsibility
- Growth

Positive motivation results from an opportunity to achieve and experience self-actualisation. The worker should have a sense of personal growth and responsibility. The theory does not always hold true. There are many cases where strong motivators can overcome poor hygiene factors.

20.4 Managing Conflict

Conflict occurs whenever two or more people disagree over something and at least one of them decides to make an issue of it. However:-

- ➤ Conflict is unavoidable
- ➤ Needs to be actively managed
- ➤ Can be beneficial

Conflict management is concerned with resolving differences of opinion that could, if unmanaged, become destructive and affect project objectives and team morale.

By the very nature of the job the project manager causes conflict:-

- ➤ By looking for trouble, omissions and mistakes
- ➤ By directing people who report to others
- ➤ By escalating problems until necessary decisions are made
- ➤ By conflicting with others' attempts to exert a dominant influence on the project

20.4.1 Conflict and the Project Life Cycle

Different phases give rise to different problems. e.g.

Concept Phase

Technical objectives not fully understood
Power struggle between PM and Functional Managers and between team members

Definition Phase

The technical solution

Execution Phase

Scheduling issues and trade offs
Technical integration issues

Closeout Phase

Schedule pressures
Personality conflicts

20.4.2 Two Party Conflict Management

The options open to people involved in a two party conflict are illustrated in the figure below.

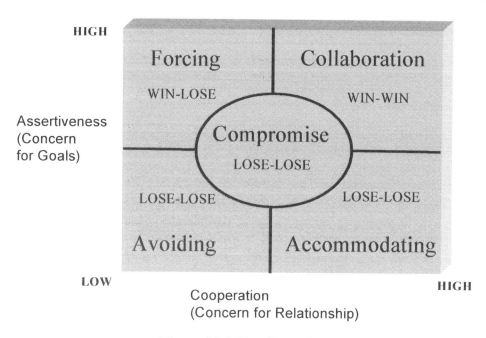

Figure 20.3 Two Party Conflict

The two dimensions considered are the Assertiveness of the parties concerned and their willingness to cooperate in resolving the issue. In general terms the only win-win solution is Collaboration but there are occasions when other approaches may be more appropriate.

20.5 Forcing

In this situation one party to the conflict has authority over the other and has imposed their preferred solution. From the point of view of the winner the problem has been solved, but at the expense of the relationship. This is a win-lose situation.

20.5.1.1   When to Force

> When quick decisive action is vital; (e.g. in emergencies).
> On important issues where unpopular actions need implementing, (e.g. in cost cutting, enforcing unpopular   rules, discipline).
> On issues vital to organisation's welfare when you know you're right.
> Against people who take advantage of non-competitive behaviour.

20.5.2   Collaboration

 In this scenario both parties together explore the best solution to the problem i.e. they confront the issue, not each other. During this process one or both parties may change their view but they both agree that the resulting solution is the best and because of this and the fact that the relationship has been maintained, or even enhanced, this is win-win.

20.5.2.1   When to Collaborate

Collaboration is usually the best option but in some situations it is particularly important.

> To find an integrative solution when both sets of concerns are too important to be compromised.
> When your objective is to learn.
> To merge insights from people with different perspectives.
> To work through feelings that may have interfered with a relationship.

20.5.3   Avoiding

This is the do nothing option. Just ignore the problem. This shows low concern for both the problem and the ongoing relationship and is a lose-lose situation because the conflict still exists.

20.5.3.1   When to Avoid

> The issue is trivial

- ➢ You see little chance of satisfaction
- ➢ The potential disruption outweighs benefits of resolution.
- ➢ To let people cool down & regain perspective.
- ➢ To gather more information
- ➢ When others can resolve the conflict more effectively

20.5.4 Accommodating

In this situation the parties wish to remain friends and therefore try and smooth over their disagreement by for instance agreeing to differ. This is still lose-lose as the underlying conflict still exists and the problem has not been solved

20.5.4.1 When to Accommodate

- ➢ When wrong – to allow a better position to be heard, to learn, show reasonableness.
- ➢ Where issues are more important to others and hence maintain co-operation.
- ➢ To build social credits for later issues.
- ➢ To minimise loss when outmatched/losing.
- ➢ If harmony and stability are very important
- ➢ To allow subordinates learn from mistakes

20.5.5 Compromising

A middle way is found that both parties can accept. Relationships are protected but this is still lose-lose because neither party gets everything they want and must give something up.

20.5.5.1 When to Compromise

- ➢ When not worth the effort or potential disruption of being more assertive
- ➢ Where opponents with equal power are committed to mutually exclusive goals
- ➢ To achieve temporary settlements to complex issues.
- ➢ To arrive at an workable solution under time pressure.

21 Health, Safety & Environmental Management

Learning Objectives

• Explain the importance of project health & safety management

• Explain the importance of project environmental management

APMP syllabus topics 2.7

21.1 Health & Safety

It is the responsibility of any managing organisation to determine and apply appropriate methods and standards and to take all appropriate steps to minimise the likelihood of accidents and injuries. Much of this responsibility falls upon the project manager. This necessitates some knowledge and understanding of the relevant health and safety regulations.

21.1.1 Health & Safety Regulations

Health & Safety at Work Act 1974

> Sets out general duties of Employers towards Staff and the Public and between Employees
> Based on "common sense" and what is reasonably practical

Management of H&S at Work Regulations 1999

> Makes it more explicit what is required to comply with 1974 Act
> Main requirement on Employers is to carry out risk assessments
> Straightforward in an office environment but can be complex when dealing with serious hazards

COSHH (Control of Substances Hazardous to Health)

The law requires Employers to carry out an 8 step process

1. Assess the risks
2. Decide what precautions are needed
3. Prevent or control exposure
4. Ensure these controls are used and maintained
5. Monitor the exposure
6. Carry out health surveillance
7. Prepare accident and emergency plans
8. Ensure employees are informed, trained and supervised

21.2 Statutory Responsibilities

21.2.1 Employers duty of care

> To provide a safe & suitable work environment
> Mental well being

- Physical well being
- Proper lighting
- Regular rest periods

21.2.2 The Responsibilities of Project Personnel

- To take reasonable care of their own health & safety and that of others who may be affected by their actions

- Cooperate with management to meet the employers legal obligation

- Not to intentionally or recklessly interfere with or misuse anything provided in the interests of health, safety or welfare

21.2.3 Statutory Requirements on a Project Manager

The project manager has a duty of care to all those involved in the project. This is a legal responsibility and obligates the project manager to:

1. Carry out a Project Risk Assessment

This concerns health and safety risk to personnel and risk to the project. The Employer, or the PM on his behalf, must ensure that all possible sources of risk are identified and appropriate measures taken to eliminate or minimise them.

2. Implement a Health & Safety Policy for the project

There should be a formal written H&S Policy for the project which states how H&S will be managed and implemented and defines roles & responsibilities. The PM must ensure that the policy is implemented

3. Facilitate training and briefing relative to Health & Safety

The PM must ensure that all project personnel receive appropriate H&S training and that measures are in place to ensure the H&S of visitors to the project locations.

4. Provide H&S reporting, review and improvement

The PM must ensure that all H&S activities are recorded and procedures are regularly reviewed and appropriate improvements made.

5. In particular all of the following must be reported to the H&S Executive

- ➢ Death or major injury
- ➢ Other injuries resulting in more than 3 days absence
- ➢ Work related diseases
- ➢ Dangerous occurrences (no injury occurs but could have done so)

21.3 Benefits of Health & Safety

Although the management of H&S can involve significant expense to the project there are substantial benefits to offset these costs:-
- ➢ There will be increased morale of the workforce
- ➢ Better industrial relations
- ➢ There will be reduced compensation claims
- ➢ Reduced probability of prosecution
- ➢ Less disruption due to accidents and sick leave
- ➢ Improved company image and reputation

21.4 Environmental factors

There are a large number of regulations pertaining to Noise & Pollution that Project Managers must comply with if relevant to the project. Much of this requires specialist knowledge so it is best to obtain professional advice.

Relevant examples include:-

- ➢ Discharges to rivers and sewers
- ➢ Avoidance of land contamination
- ➢ Control, storage and disposal of waste
- ➢ Noise conditions set out in planning approval
- ➢ Air pollution, solvent emissions, waste incineration
- ➢ Disposal of plant, equipment, machinery and vehicles

22 Handover & Closeout

Learning Objectives

•Understand the importance of formal project handover and closeout

•Describe the activities involved in handover & closeout

APMP syllabus topics 6.5, 6.6(part)

22.1 Handover

Handover consists of all those activities involved with the formal transfer of ownership from the project team to the client/sponsor and end users. It could be a simple handover of product and documentation or a more lengthy process involving testing and training.

The process must demonstrate that the deliverables conform to the specified performance requirements. The handover process must be planned and documented in the project plan.

- Handover must be formal and recorded to ensure transfer over of responsibilities and ownership
- Products/facilities must be subject to pre-agreed acceptance tests
- All pertinent documentation must be signed off
- A process must be in place to handle any outstanding problems e.g snags/bugs
- Terms and conditions of warranties and maintenance must be agreed and documented.

22.1.1   A Handover Process

1. Prepare the Handover Plan. This should be agreed with the Client. It will define all the steps of the handover process, roles and responsibilities and acceptance criteria and any ongoing support and training requirements.

2. Preparation and testing of deliverables by the project team prior to formal handover. This is to ensure that the handover will go smoothly.

3. Carry out acceptance tests with the Client and users. These tests will be those previously agreed with the client end user representatives.

4. Document results of tests and if satisfactory transfer responsibility and formal ownership. If the tests are not satisfactory the process may have to be stopped whist remedial actions take place.

5. Agree and document outstanding issues regarding bug fixes/snagging lists. Even though the deliverables may pass Acceptance there will probably still be minor outstanding issues

6. Hand over all deliverables and transfer responsibility and formal ownership.

22.2 Closeout

Closeout is concerned with closing the project down in a consistent and organised manner. It should include all the following activities.

- ➢ Tidying up and archiving of project files
  - ○ All project documentation must be sorted, filed and indexed to facilitate later retrieval to cover issues such as Technical, Financial, Legal, Copyright, IPR etc
- ➢ Financial Accounting
  - ○ All monies received and paid
  - ○ All costs and revenues reconciled to baseline budget plus changes
  - ○ All surplus stocks and equipment properly disposed of
- ➢ Staff
  - ○ Staff demobilised and appropriate feedback given
  - ○ Recognition of individual and team performance
  - ○ Appropriate staff retained/obtained to cover warranties and maintenance
- ➢ Closeout meetings
  - ○ Formal closeout meetings held with Client and sub contractors to ensure that all outstanding issues have been addressed
- ➢ Prepare for Post Project Review

22.3 Post Project Review

The post-project review evaluates the project against its success criteria. Its primary aim is to ensure that lessons learnt can be applied to improve the strategy, planning and management of future projects.

- ➢ The post project review occurs after handover of the project deliverables i.e. all work completed and signed off.
- ➢ It is the management review at the end of the project and does not consider the technical issues.
- ➢ The PM is responsible for ensuring it takes place but should not lead it. This should be done by an independent facilitator
- ➢ It should be a non-confrontational meeting. Its purpose is not to allocate blame

22.3.1   Agenda

- ➢ History of the project
- ➢ Performance of the project organisation
- ➢ Accuracy of project planning and estimating Reasons behind variances between plan and actual
- ➢ Suitability of monitoring and control systems
- ➢ Suitability of the project strategy for the option selected in the investment appraisal

It does not consider benefits realisation. This is the subject of the future Post Implementation Review and is the responsibility of the sponsor.

22.3.2　Planning considerations

Things to consider when planning a Post Project Review

- ➤ Who will facilitate it?
- ➤ Who should be present?
- ➤ Where will it take place?
- ➤ When and how long?
- ➤ How will the agenda be organised?
- ➤ Who will record the conclusions and lessons learned and produce the report?
- ➤ How will the lessons learned be disseminated?

22.3.3　Sources of information

Rather than rely on memory it is better to have project information to hand, preferentially in electronic form.

- ➤ Business case
- ➤ Project Plan
- ➤ Earned Value Reports
- ➤ Status Reports
- ➤ Risk and Issues Log
- ➤ Change Log
- ➤ Minutes of meetings
- ➤ Results of reviews
- ➤ Audit reports
- ➤ Correspondence

23 Revision Questions

For obvious reasons APM do not make public their examination questions. However they do publish sample questions of the kind to be expected. For copyright reasons it is not permissible to reproduce these questions here but they can be downloaded at http://www.apm.org.uk/APMP.asp along with the exam syllabus and candidate guidance notes.

23.1 General guidance

APMP exam questions usually stipulate how many separate points need to be made. So if it says make 5 points then structure your answer as 5 separate and distinct paragraphs rather than 1 solid block of text. Make sure that your answer has each point clearly numbered so that the marker is in no doubt that you have fully addressed the question.

Make sure you read the candidate guidance notes from the APM website and fully understand the following terms used in the examination.

- List
    - A simple list without explanation
- State
    - A single sentence of explanation
- Describe
    - A paragraph of 2 or 3 sentences
- Explain
    - Also at least 2 sentences but may also require diagrams and specific examples.

The paper contains 16 questions and you are expected to answer 10 in 3 hours. If more are attempted only the first 10 will be marked.

Control your time and initially allow 15 minutes per question. Move on after this time unless you are very close to finishing.

Start each question on a new page and leave space to add extra content later on if you have the time. Write on 1 side of the page only.

Make sure all questions are clearly numbered and do it as you go along. You will not be allowed time at the end to do this and unclear questions may be disregarded.

Avoid essay style answers. Make your points briefly and avoid padding. Make use of bullet points, especially if running out of time.

It can still be difficult to know how much to write therefore you must timebox your answers. Leave space and if you find you have time left over at the end you can always go back and add more material.

What follows are revision questions which are comparable in style and level of difficulty to those found in the real APMP examination. Each question is worth 50 marks giving a maximum of 500 marks. Traditionally the pass mark was 60% or 300 marks. However APM no longer publish a pass mark.

The example answers that follow are not claimed to be "perfect" answers, nor are they the only valid answers. Other answers may be equally as valid.

Some of the questions can be answered with a virtually a direct copy of the course materials. Others will require interpretation and/or extension of the course materials. Most questions will involve a single topic but some will cross topic boundaries.

23.2 Practice revision questions

1 Projects, Programmes and Portfolios

1) Explain the terms Programme Management and Portfolio Management and give examples of 3 key differences between them.

2) Explain the benefits of grouping connected projects under the overall control of a Programme Manager rather than as isolated initiatives. Make 5 distinct points.

2 Project Context

1) Explain what you understand by the term "project context" and describe 4 possible examples of project context.

2) Explain the term "Environmental Impact Analysis" and describe 2 tools you might use to carry out such an analysis

3 Project Organisation

1) Explain the strengths and weaknesses of using a matrix structure compared with other options for organising project teams. You should make 5 points.

2) List 5 roles involved with the management and execution of a typical project and describe their responsibilities

4 Project Governance & Methodology

1) Explain 5 benefits that would accrue to an organisation that practiced good governance of projects.

2a) State the 6 principles of the governance of project management. (30 marks)

2b) For any 2 of the above explain the possible consequences of failing to abide by them. (20 marks)

5 Project Life Cycles and Reviews

1) Explain 5 benefits of a project life cycle

2) Explain a project life cycle that you are familiar with by describing which key activities occur within each stage or phase.

6 The Business Case

1a Explain 2 reasons why it is important for the Sponsor to own the Business Case for a project. (20 marks)

1b. Describe 3 techniques for investment appraisal. (30 marks)

2. Describe 5 drawbacks or limitations of investment appraisal techniques

7 Managing Stakeholders

1. With the aid of a diagram describe a process that can be used to analyse stakeholders, and explain the benefits of such a process. Make 4 relevant points.

2a State what is meant by a stakeholder and describe the importance of Stakeholder Management (10 marks)

2b Describe 4 different types of stakeholder and give a real life example for each. (40 marks)

8 Success and Benefits Management, & Requirements Management

1. Explain 5 uses of success criteria and or key performance indicators (KPIs) during the lifetime of the project

2. Explain the purpose of requirements management. Make5 points

9 The Project Management Plan

1. Explain 5 different tasks that a project manager would take responsibility for in the preparation of the project management plan.

2. Explain any 5 of the topics you might expect to find in a Project Management Plan.

10 Scope Management

1. Explain 5 benefits arising out of the use of a work breakdown structures when planning and controlling a project.

2a. Explain why it is necessary to control scope on a project. (10 marks)

2b. Define 4 steps that are required to produce a detailed scope definition starting with the Business Plan.

11 Estimating

1a. Explain why estimating accuracy increases over the project life cycle. (10 marks)
1b. Explain 3 different estimating techniques. (40 marks)

2. Explain with the aid of a diagram the technique known as 3 point estimating and discuss its relevance to risk assessment.

12 Scheduling & Resource Management

1. Fully analyse the network below. Indicate the critical path and state which activities have free float and how much. What happens to the critical path if B is delayed by 5?

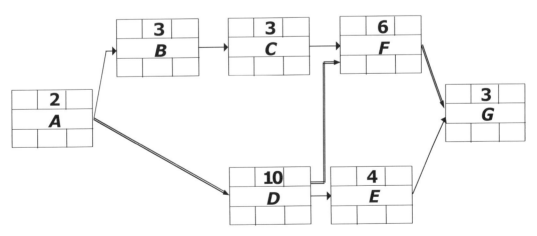

2. Convert the above network into a Gantt chart. The chart should clearly indicate Total Float and Free Float.

13 Managing Risks and Issues

1. Draw a diagram to illustrate the Risk Management process and use it to explain a process for managing threats.

2a. From the grid below identify the top 4 risks. (10 marks)

2b State 4 appropriate responses to these risks. (20 marks)

2c State 4 generic actions that a project manager would take in planning a response to a particular risk. (20 marks)

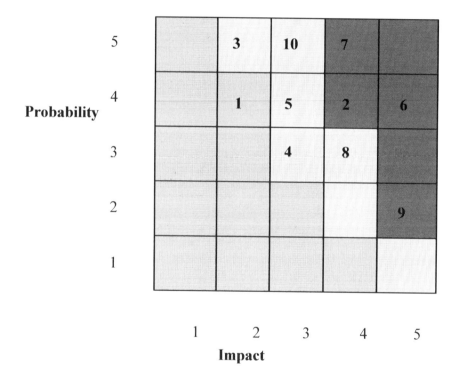

14 Quality Management

1. Describe the purpose of project quality management (10 marks). Describe 4 key processes in quality management (40 marks).

2. Explain how a project manager would ensure the quality requirements are achieved during the project. Make 5 points.

15 Change Control & Configuration Management

1. Explain a typical change control process, making 5 substantial points.

2. Define what is meant by Configuration Management (10 marks)
    State the 5 principal activities that make up configuration management.(40 marks)

16 Budgeting, Cost Management & Earned Value

1. Explain why it is necessary to budget and manage costs in a project (10 marks).
   Describe 4 types of cost information needed to manage project costs (40 marks).

2. A project is being monitored using the earned value method, has a budget of   £100,000
   and is planned to complete in 12 months. The following table shows the situation at the end
   of month 5.

Month	Planned Value £K	Earned Value £K	Actual Value £K
1	10	5	10
2	20	15	25
3	30	35	40
4	40	40	50
5	50	45	60

At the end of month 5 ……………..

a) What are the values of cost variance and schedule variance?
   State the meaning of these terms.

b) What would you estimate the cost at completion to be, making 2 different assumptions
about future cost performance?

c) Estimate the completion time, again making 2 different assumptions?

17 Communications & Information Management

1. State 10 practices that a Project Manager should adopt in order to facilitate effective
project communication.

2. Explain 5 factors a project manager should consider when developing a communication
plan.

18 Procurement & Negotiation

1. List 5 different contract types/payment structures that you are familiar with and describe for each the situation they would be most appropriate for.

2. List the 5 stages of negotiation and describe the main elements of each stage.

19 Teamwork

1. As a project manager you have inherited an established project team. Explain 5 examples of good practice that you would use to facilitate effective team working.

2. Explain the 5 stages of team development.

20 Leadership & Conflict Management

1. Describe 5 characteristics of a good leader

2. Explain 5 different approaches to managing conflict and for each one describe a situation where it might be appropriate.

21 Health, Safety & Environmental Management

1. Explain 5 actions required of the project manager on behalf of the employer that must be taken to comply with Health and Safety legislation.(40 marks)
What are the benefits to the organisation? (10 marks)

2. Explain the overall aim of the Health and Safety at Work Act, 1974 (10 marks). Explain 4 specific duties of care upon employers regarding health and safety at work (50 marks).

22 Handover & Closeout

1. Explain an effective handover process.

2. Explain 5 things a project manager should consider when planning the post project review.

23.3 Revision question answers

1   Projects, Programmes and Portfolios

1) *Explain the terms Programme Management and Portfolio Management and give examples of 3 key differences between them.*

Programme Management is the co-ordinated management of a group of projects that are inter-related and/or interdependent and contribute to a common strategic objective. They are all individually project managed but all project managers report to the overall Programme Manager. Programme Management is a strategic tool that links Corporate objectives to projects

A Portfolio is defined as the totality of all an organisation's programmes, projects and related operational activities. It ensures the integration of projects and programmes with Operations. Portfolio management is particularly concerned with the management of resources across competing projects and programmes with particular regard to:-

- Scarce or limited resources and capacity bottlenecks
- Balance across the portfolio between risk and return
- Timing of the project i.e. when it takes place

Key Differences

1. Projects in a Programme are always inter-related and interdependent and all contribute to the same overall corporate objective. Projects in a Portfolio can have no dependencies apart from possible resource conflicts.
2. Projects in a Programme all contribute to the same defined strategic objective. A portfolio can support several strategic objectives.
3. In a Programme all projects must usually succeed for the programme to totally succeed whereas in a Portfolio failures in some areas can be compensated by successes in other projects. Meeting overall portfolio goals is more important than the success of individual portfolio elements.

----

2) *Explain the benefits of grouping connected projects under the overall control of a Programme Manager rather than as isolated initiatives. Make 5 distinct points.*

1. All projects must in some way contribute to overall organisational objectives. Managing projects as a coordinated programme under the control of a programme manager will help ensure that project goals are aligned with those objectives.

2. Having an overall programme manager with responsibility for related projects will ensure the best allocation of shared resources. Resource conflicts can be managed and prioritised to the benefit of the overall programme rather than individual projects. Expensive resources can be shared in the most cost effective manner.

3. Within a programme, projects will typically have dependencies and interdependencies on other projects. Managing them as a programme allows the interfaces to be managed and all project activities coordinated to the needs of the programme. Managing project interfaces is a key programme manager responsibility.

4. Projects usually involve risk. Total risk can best be managed and mitigated by controlling it at programme level rather than at project level. For instance a risk to the schedule for an individual project may have no impact at programme level.

5. Projects can often produce solutions which whilst benefiting a specific area may actual harm organisational goals. Programme management can involve the whole value chain and avoid sub optimal solutions.

----

2 Project Context

1) Explain what you understand by the term "project context" and describe 4 possible examples of project context.

Projects do not take place in a vacuum. They take place within a "context" or "environment" and the successful accomplishment of a project generally requires a significant sensitivity to, and appreciation of, the context in which it is based. Contextual elements can be found both internal and external to the project.

Internal examples

1) The governance environment in which the project takes place. This includes company and project standards, methods, policies, procedures and methodologies.

2) The availability and quality of internal resources including human, physical and financial resources. If sufficient internal resources are not available then it may be necessary to look outside the organisation

External examples

1) The political and economic environment. This includes factors such as inflation rates, interest rates, economic outlook, legislation, government policies. All of these can affect the success of the project.

2) The competition. What are your competitors doing that may adversely impact the success of your project? Competitor activity can adversely affect the output, timing and success of your project.

----

2) Explain the term "Environmental Impact Analysis" and describe 2 tools you might use to carry out such an analysis giving examples where appropriate.

An Environmental Impact Analysis is an exercise carried out early in the project life cycle to determine factors, both internal and external to the project/organisation that may impact its success. It is a component of Risk Analysis and will uncover threats and opportunities pertaining to the project. It is typically a joint responsibility of the Sponsor and the Project Manager.

Generally the Sponsor will take most responsibility for external factors and the Project Manager for internal factors.

Two tools

1.PESTLE analysis

PESTLE is an acronym that stands for:-

> **P**olitical
> **E**conomic
> **S**ociological
> **T**echnological
> **L**egal / Regulatory
> **E**thical/Environmental

It is simply a tool for providing some structure to the analysis. Possible examples under each of the headings are as follows:-

- **Political**
  - Taxation
  - Government Policies
- **Economic**
  - Interest rates
  - Economic outlook
- **Social**
  - Current Fashions
  - Demographics

- **Technology**
  - eCommerce
  - Leading edge
- **Legal**
  - Employment law
  - Environmental regulations
- **Ethical**
  - Job losses
  - 3rd world exploitation

2. SWOT analysis

SWOT stands for Strengths, Weaknesses, Opportunities and Threats. It is another useful tool for studying both the internal and external environments of projects or of organisations. Strengths and weaknesses will generally be found more within the internal environment.

Examples are product and project portfolios, production facilities, staff, IT systems etc. Opportunities and threats generally arise from the external environment.

Both PESTLE and SWOT analyses are best carried out by "Brainstorming" using members of the project team and appropriate stakeholders.

SWOT analysis can be carried out at any level of detail ranging from a whole organisation to a sub-project or product.

----

3 Project Organisation

1) Explain the strengths and weaknesses of using a matrix structure compared with other options for organising project teams. You should make 5 points.

Strengths

1. **Expertise and use of resources.** Because a matrix organization is cross-functional one of its strengths is that it can call upon the skills and expertise of all the Functions and because resources are all owned by the Functions, it is easier to use them as and when required and to share resources between different projects, leading to more efficient use of resource.

2. **Line Management.** Because team members still have functional managers the PM does not have the added responsibility and workload of line management. Also he does not have to worry about end of project deployment as resources simply return to their functional manager

Weaknesses

3. **Functional conflicts and loyalties.** There may be conflict between people from different functions, especially if things start to go wrong on the project. Also team members know that ultimately their line manager has the greatest influence on their career progression therefore that may influence their behaviour.

4. **Communications.** Because of the need to communicate across function as well as within the project, communications in a matrix organisation are always more complex than in functional or projectised structures

Both

5. **Power of the Project Manager.** In a matrix structure the PM usually has considerably more power than in a Functional structure, especially in a strong matrix organisation. However he will probably not exercise the same amount of power as that in a fully projectised structure.

2) List 5 roles involved with the management and execution of a typical project and describe their responsibilities

1 Project Sponsor

      Makes the business case for the project and obtain expenditure approval
      Chairs the Project Board and provide the link up to Senior Management
      Makes sure business benefits are realised
      Carries out phase reviews
      Determines the relative priority of Time, Cost & Quality

2 Project Manager

      Building, organising, motivating and managing the project team
      Integrating human, financial and physical resources
      Planning and leading the work of the project
      Monitoring and controlling project execution
      Reporting and communicating with stakeholders

3 Project Team Members

      Assist and advise the project manager with regard to planning within their area of expertise
      Take responsibility for individual work packages
      Carry out the instructions of the project manager
      Keep the project manager informed of progress and issues
      Communicate and cooperate with other team members

4 End Users

      Assist in defining project requirements
      Be involved in devising acceptance criteria and tests
      Keep involved with the project as it evolves

5 Quality Assurance

      Carry out quality assurance audits in line with corporate policies
      Report audit outcomes to the project board/sponsor
      Ensure correction of any quality assurance issues

----

4 Project Governance & Methodology

1. Explain 5 benefits that would accrue to an organisation that practiced good governance of projects.

1) Projects must be financially and technically justified through a defined approval process. This means that there is far less likelihood of executing projects that will ultimately fail due to financial, technical or marketing problems. Also no single person or small group can force through unsuitable projects.

2) The Project portfolio is aligned to Corporate goals and strategies. This eliminates the possibility of taking on projects that may not contribute to corporate objectives or may conflict with other projects or programmes. It will also help ensure that resources are not wasted on such projects to the detriment of others.

3) Projects are controlled at a high level via ongoing reviews. This scrutiny ensures that projects are less likely to go out of control and when necessary projects can be terminated if they are no longer viable.

4) Lessons learned from ongoing projects can be fed back into the organisation. This leads to avoidance of repeating mistakes and improved performance of future projects.

5) The interests of directors, project staff, stockholders and other stakeholders are aligned. This leads to a climate of trust and openness, less surprises and more predictable performance

----

2 a) State 6 principles of the governance of project management.

1. Projects should be clearly linked to key business objectives
2. There should be clear senior management ownership of project
3. There should be effective engagement with stakeholders
4. Leaders must have the required project and risk management skills
5. There should be appropriate contact at senior level with key suppliers
6. Projects should be driven by long term value rather than short term cost
7. Projects should be broken down into manageable steps
(select any 6)

b) For any 2 of the above explain the possible consequences of failing to abide by them.

1. Projects should be clearly linked to key business objectives. All properly run organisations set themselves objectives. The actions required to meet those objectives will usually generate

projects and programmes. Projects consume financial, technical and human resources and most organisations do not have the capability to carry out all the projects they would like to do. Therefore it follows that if projects are taking place that are not related to business objectives than those objectives are put at risk.

2. There should be appropriate contact at senior level with key suppliers

When projects involve 3rd party suppliers then this represents a significant project risk. Your project is not as important to them as it is to you and unless they see you as a key customer you may not get the service you expect. Deliveries may be late and/or of poor quality. This risk can be mitigated by having contacts at senior level. Although the project manager will handle day to day issues it is much easier to resolve problems if there is direct communication between senior managers.

----

5 Project Life Cycles and Reviews

1) Explain 5 benefits of a project life cycle

Benefits of having a project life cycle and hence cutting projects into separate phases are:-

1. By having smaller chunks the projects are **easier to manage and control**. By looking just at the current phase it helps us concentrate on the immediate problems so that we do the right work in the right order.

2. By concentrating on the current phase it facilitates **rolling wave planning**. Rolling wave planning is where the work immediately in front of us is planned in detail, down to task level, whilst work in future phases is not yet fully defined.

3. It facilitates **more accurate estimating**. Estimating is always more accurate with smaller chunks of work so estimating by phase will be more accurate than by a total top down approach. Each phase can be estimated separately and can be combined with rolling wave planning.

4. Each phase end gives management an opportunity to review the project so far, see how it is performing and still meeting the business case. These are sometimes called **Gateway reviews**. They enable good project to receive continuing management endorsement whilst poorly performing projects can receive management attention and perhaps termination.

5. **Risks can be contained** within each phase. Risk management is a continuous process. Although risk analysis must be carried out at the start of the project the Gateway reviews must include a revised risk analysis utilizing the experience and knowledge gained from the previous phase.

2. Explain a project life cycle that you are familiar with by describing which key activities occur within each stage or phase.

Shown below is a generic lifecycle which can be applied to many different kinds of project.

In the **Concept** phase the need/problem/opportunity emerges and the proposed solution is tested for technical and financial feasibility. At this stage plans may be at a very low level of details and estimates of costs and timescales are at a low level of accuracy. Plans only need to be accurate enough to decide whether the project is worth continuing into the next phase. This phase will produce the Business Plan.

The **Definition** phase is where detailed plans are formulated. A Work Breakdown Structure will be created and the project scheduled and costed in order to arrive at a budget. Risk analysis will take place. Resources will be agreed. Monitoring tools will be put in place. This stage will produce a detailed Project Management Plan.

The **Implementation** stage is where most of the work takes place and the project deliverables are produced. This stage is often broken down into further sub-phases. The project work will be monitored and controlled using such tools as Earned Value Management, Risk Management and Change Control.

Handover to the Client takes place when the project deliverables have been completed and Acceptance Tests have been successfully completed.

Closeout phase formally **closes** the project down. All project documentation is sorted and filed and financial accounting completed. Staff will be demobilised and a final closeout meeting held. The project will conclude with a post project review.

----

6 The Business Case

1a: Explain 2 reasons why it is important for the Sponsor to own the Business Case for a project.

1. The project manager will usually hand over responsibility for the project when the deliverables have been formally accepted. At this stage the business benefits, defined in the

business case, have yet to be realised. As the sponsor owns the benefits realisation he should also be responsible for making the business case for the project.

2. The sponsor provides the link between the project and senior management. Senior management determine corporate objectives. Every project must be aligned to corporate objectives hence the sponsor is best placed to ensure that the business case supports corporate objectives.

1b: Describe 3 techniques for investment appraisal.

1. Payback

This method calculates how long it takes for cash flow to break even; i.e. when costs equal benefits. This method ignores cash flows after break-even point. It can be used to compare projects to see which one returns the initial investment soonest, thus freeing cash for further investment. Longer payback times represent increased risk.

2. Net Present Value (NPV)

Payback ignores the fact that the value of money diminishes over time. NPV works by discounting each annual cash amount to its value in today's money. Effectively it is the reverse of compound interest. Summing the individual discounted values gives a single figure which represents the project value in today's terms. It can be used to evaluate individual projects and to compare projects.

3. Internal Rate of Return (IRR)

NPV requires us to select a rate to discount at. The difficulties of selecting an appropriate discount rate can be overcome if we turn the problem around. Instead of selecting a rate and then seeing if the project is profitable at that rate we can work out what the rate would have to be make the discounted costs and benefits of the project equal each other. In other words what rate would produce a NPV of zero? The value obtained represents the IRR. This can be used to compare projects and also to determine if the rate is acceptable for the risk involved.
----

2. Describe 5 drawbacks or limitations of investment appraisal techniques

1. Accuracy of estimates

Investment Appraisal involves forecasting the future. This could involve forecasting sales revenues, efficiency savings, productivity improvements etc. These values are arrived at by the expertise and judgement of the people involved but they are just estimates and they will invariably be wrong.

2 Bias and unrealistic expectations

On any project there will be those in favour and those against. Those in favour will10d to stress the benefits and try and minimise the potential costs and those against will do the reverse. Many projects are approved based on unrealistic expectations.

3 Strategic Considerations

It is often necessary to take on projects which are not profitable, for strategic reasons. It may be necessary to defend a market position or to open new markets or to improve prospects of future business.

4 Legislation

New rules and regulations are constantly being imposed on organisations. They usually involve health and safety or environmental considerations. They have to be obeyed regardless of cost unless the organisation withdraws from the affected operations.

5 Intangible costs

Not all costs or benefits can be expressed in terms of money. Many beneficial projects can not be justified on cash terms. The main benefits can arise in improving quality of life, for example building a hospital or a bypass. The same can apply to costs e.g social costs of noise and air pollution due to new motorway.

----

7 Managing Stakeholders

1. With the aid of a diagram describe a process that can be used to analyse stakeholders, and explain the benefits of such a process. Make 4 relevant points.

1. Identify all significant stakeholders. This can be done as a team exercise and the information collected either as a simple list or on a chart showing how the stakeholders relate to each other.

2. Analyse each stakeholder in terms of attitude to the project, their motivation and expectations and their ability to influence.
The following tool could be used to aid this process.

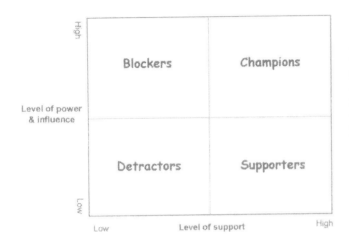

Blockers are people who do not support the project and have the power to cause harm.
Detractors also do not support the project but have little power.
Supporters are in favour but also have little power
Champions want the project to succeed and have the power to help.

Having done this it should then be possible to formulate an action plan to bring them or keep them on your side. A table such as the following could capture this information.

Stakeholder	Attitude/Power	Motivation	Action Plan

3 The ongoing stage of the process is to continuously monitor and control the situation. As the project progresses through its lifecycle new stakeholders may appear and others may change their positions so the position must be continuously monitored.

4 The main benefits arising out of stakeholder management:-

- It will help identify risks and opportunities that may otherwise have not been exposed.
- It means that stakeholder issues can be treated in a proactive rather than reactive fashion.
- It facilitates the understanding of stakeholder expectations and hence makes those expectations easier to manage.
- Because of the above 3 facts there is an enhanced probability of project success.

2a State what is meant by a stakeholder and describe the importance of Stakeholder Management

A Stakeholder is defined as any person or body that has an interest in a project or its outcome or is affected by it. The attitude and actions of Stakeholders can have a significant effect on the performance and outcome of your project and hence they must be proactively managed. The influence of stakeholders must be considered right at the start of the project when preparing the business case. It is particularly important to recognise and manage negative stakeholders as if left unmanaged they can have a detrimental effect on the project.

2b List 4 different types of stakeholder and give a real life example for each.

1. People and Organisations who may be directly affected by the project

An example of this is the building of a bypass around a village. Some people will be positively affected as it will reduce congestion and pollution in the village but businesses may be disadvantaged by loss of passing trade

2. People and Organisations not directly affected but who may have strong opinions about the project, either positive or negative.

An example of this is a construction project that destroys habitat such as building a runway or a reservoir. People who live nowhere near the projects will object on environmental possibly through such groups as Greenpeace or Friends of the Earth.

3. Statutory and regulatory bodies

An example of this could be the construction of an industrial plant where Government and local regulations will impose stringent health & safety, environmental and planning regulations.

4. Potential end users of the project products

An example of this is the introduction of a new IT system. There is a natural resistance to change and end user expectations must be managed and their cooperation obtained by involving them in the project requirements and solution design.

----

8 Success & Benefits Management, & Requirements Management

1. Explain 5 uses of success criteria and or key performance indicators in the planning and management of projects

1. Success factors and KPI's should be developed during the business case. The represent a consensus amongst stakeholders as to what constitutes success and how it is measured. They can help justify the investment.

2. They provide focus for the planning of the project and the setting of realistic objectives. In particular they can help prioritise the 3 key criteria of time, cost & quality when progress deviates from the plan.

3. During phase reviews the success criteria and associated KPI's can be used to help determine if the project is on track to meet its objectives and can then help to drive any corrections.

4. When significant changes are proposed they can be evaluated for their affect on the success factors. This may result in the changes being refused or in extreme cases if the change is deemed essential it may cause the project to be aborted due to an inability to now meet the success criteria.

5. During Handover & Closeout and later at the Benefits Review they can be used to demonstrate or otherwise the overall success of the project.

----

2. Explain the purpose of requirements management. Make 5 points

1. To Capture requirements
Requirements are captured mainly by interviewing relevant stakeholders. It is necessary to gain a wide spectrum of opinions to make sure that all possible requirements are captured.

2. Analysis of the requirements
The gathered requirements must be tested for feasibility, validity, compatibility, acceptability, applicability and consistency. It is often found that some of the requirements of different stakeholders are mutually exclusive or are very difficult to provide. All such issues must be cleared before finalising the requirements. If necessary the Sponsor must act as referee.

3. Prioritising of requirements
It is often not possible to include all the requirements into time and budget constraints. It is therefore usual to prioritise the requirements and exclude some of them from the project scope. Here again the Sponsor may have to referee.

4. Design of Acceptance Tests
Once the requirements have been agreed acceptance rests must be devised and agreed. They are best done at this stage rather than at completion because they clarify understanding of the requirements and will often cause them to be modified. **Acceptance tests are best devised by potential end users under the guidance of the** project team.

5. Production of a Functional Specification
Requirements are documented in a Functional Specification. This document captures all the agreed user requirements in an unambiguous manner. It defines what is required but not how the requirement will be met. As its name implies it describes the functions of the system.

9 The Project Management Plan

1. Explain 5 different tasks that a project manager would take responsibility for in the preparation of the project management plan.

1. Understand the Business Case
Ideally the project manager should work with the Sponsor to produce the Business Case and agree the outline budget and schedule and Key Performance Indicators. However in many cases the PM is not appointed at this stage. In that situation the PM should study the business case and discuss any issues with the Sponsor.

2. Scope Definition
Building on the Business Case the PM should define:
- what has to be achieved
- project scope
- success criteria
- project deliverables
- constraints and assumptions

3. Define the work by developing a WBS
With the help of the project team the PM must break down the work of the project into suitably sized work packages.

4. Estimate and Schedule each work package.
Again using the project team the PM will estimate the cost, duration and resource requirements for each work package and then schedule the work to determine the planned duration, budget and critical path.

5. Carry out Risk Analysis
Using appropriate stakeholders and team members the PM will carry out a risk analysis and produce a risk management plan. The output of this process may mean changes to the budget and/or schedule.

----

2. Explain any 5 of the topics you might expect to find in a Project Management Plan.

1. A Work Breakdown Structure. (WBS)

A WBS will define all the work necessary to carry out the project down to task level. It defines the project scope and is the basis for building the schedule and the budget. It is a hierarchical structure with the work broken down level by level until specific tasks have been defined, usually of about 1 to 2 weeks duration.

2 A Project Schedule

The schedule is the project timetable. All the tasks identified on the WBS can be put onto a time schedule once their dependencies have been established. The schedule can be represented by a network diagram or by a Gantt chart. Either method will show the earliest and latest times that each activity can take place. The sequence of activities that determine the overall project duration is known as the critical path

3. Project Budget

Each task on the schedule will have a planned cost. The planned costs for each time period can be established from the schedule. They can then be accumulated to determine the S-curve for the project. This is known as the Budgeted Cost of Work Scheduled (BCWS) and is the basis for controlling the budget

4. Stakeholder Management Plan

This plan will establish who the principal project stakeholders are. For each stakeholder, or stakeholder group, it will establish their disposition, their motivation and a plan of action. This will enable the project manager to adopt a proactive mode. Principal stakeholders include the Client/Sponsor, the end users, the project team and suppliers & partners.

5. Roles & Responsibilities

Each team member and principal stakeholders will have their roles and responsibilities clearly defined so that every one knows exactly what is expected of them. For project team members their work is defined on the WBS but can more conveniently be represented by a Responsibility Matrix.

----

10 Scope Management

1. Explain 5 benefits arising out of the use of a work breakdown structures when planning and controlling a project.

1. Its production facilitates team building
Because the WBS must cover all the work of the project it requires input from the entire project team. This is best done as a team activity. A spin off benefit is that the act of building the WBS as a team helps build team spirit and morale and gets the team "buy in" to the plan.

2. It focuses attention on project objectives and deliverables

Each work package will have a measurable deliverable. These deliverables will combine to form the overall project deliverables and objectives. Hence the whole process is focussed on what work must be done to meet the project objectives.

3. It forces detailed planning

Production of the WBS is a top down process which stops at an appropriate level of detail. Hence the process forces the team to plan in detail and makes it less likely to mistakenly leave something out.

4. It facilitates the allocation of responsibility for individual packets of work

Each work package identified on the WBS will bear the name of the person responsible for its completion. Thus the responsibility for each piece of work is clearly stated.

5. The WBS is the foundation on which the whole project is built. It is the starting point for all the processes that follow e.g

- Budgeting
- Estimating
- Scheduling
- Controlling
- Change Control
- Configuration Management

2a. Explain why it is necessary to control scope on a project. (10 marks)

Scope Management is concerned with all the tools and processes that ensure that enough work, but no more, is carried out to produce the project deliverables. It is concerned with controlling the boundaries of the project and ensuring that all work done is related to project objectives and that any new work is subject to a formal change control process. Failure to control scope will result in unplanned work resulting in failure to meet project objectives.

2b. Define 4 steps that are required to produce a detailed scope definition starting with the Business Plan.

Step 1
The Business Plan will have specified the end products of the project (e.g the final deliverables).Identifying these deliverables is the starting point for scope definition.

Step 2

This step involves breaking down the final deliverables into intermediate products. This will involve not just physical products but also associated documentation.

Step 3

This involves determining the work required to produce each intermediate product and if necessary breaking the work down into smaller work packages.

Step 4

The 4th step is to estimate for each work package the cost, resource requirements and duration. If all the work has been properly defined then the aggregation of all the work packages in terms of costs and resources will represent the scope of the project.

----

11 Estimating

1a. Explain why estimating accuracy increases over the project life cycle.

- At the start of a project accurate estimates are difficult due to lack of information.
- Accuracy improves as planning activities start.
- More detailed planning produces better estimates
- As we start work on the Implementation we see how good the estimates are and we can re-estimate the future work
- Nearing the end of the project estimates are very accurate as they are based on experience and hindsight

This concept is known as the Estimating Funnel

1b. Explain 3 different estimating techniques.

1 Bottom Up Estimating

This method is based on the WBS. All the individual lower level tasks in the WBS are estimated independently and then rolled up to produce the project estimates. This is a laborious method and its accuracy is dependant on having a correct WBS. However it is the most accurate way of estimating. It is sometimes known as the definitive estimate.

2 Comparative Estimating

This is also called Top Down or Historic estimating. It simply involves using experience from similar projects carried out in the past. It takes the overall costs and timescales for similar projects and adjusts them for size and complexity. The danger is that previous projects may have been inefficient and/or badly managed. Comparative estimating can also be used at task level to support bottom up.

3 Parametric Estimating

Parametric estimating uses a mathematical model or formulae to produce project estimates based on input parameters. It is usually based on historical data. Simple examples are square metres in construction and lines of code in software development. Quantity Surveyors make extensive use of parametric estimating.

----

2. Explain with the aid of a diagram the technique known as 3 point estimating and discuss its relevance to risk assessment.

 3 point estimating recognises the uncertainty in the estimating process and attempts to set upper and lower bounds to the estimates as well as a most expected value.

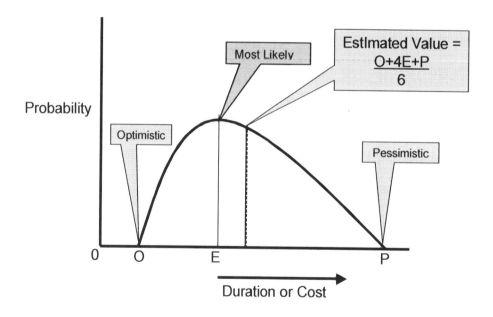

Instead of developing a single estimate we estimate a best possible "optimistic" time, the highest likely "pessimistic" time, worst case scenario, and what is believed to be the "expected" or best estimate. Experience has shown that by asking for 3 estimates rather than 1 the expected value obtained is a better estimate than just asking for a single value.

The technique can also be used for the estimated costs.

The single value we use for the estimate is calculated by using the "PERT" formulae:

Estimated Value = (Optimistic + 4*Expected + Pessimistic)/6

Because the distribution is normally skewed to the right this value will usually be higher then the original expected value. This technique will lead to a longer critical path than would otherwise be the case, leading to a more realistic schedule.

By identifying lower and upper bounds for each activity we are effectively measuring the schedule risk for each activity. All the 3 point estimates for a project can be utilised by Monte Carlo Simulation. This will produce a probability distribution of the expected project duration and budget thus measuring time and cost risk for the whole project.

----

12 Scheduling

1. Fully analyse the network below. Indicate the critical path and state which activities have free float and how much. What happens to the critical path if B is delayed by 5?

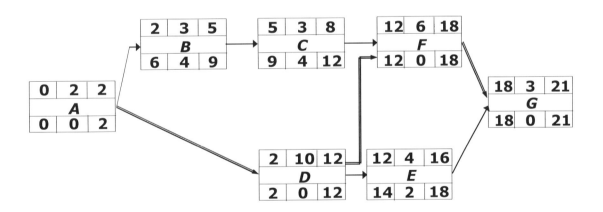

Free Float   E=2,   C= 4,

The Critical Path is ADFG which is 21 long.   Path ABCFG =2+3+3+6+3=17.
If B is delayed by 5 then this path increases to 22 and becomes the new critical path.

----

2. Convert the network into a Gantt chart. The chart should clearly indicate Total Float and Free Float.

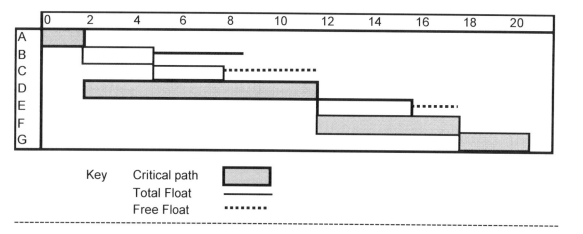

Key	Critical path	▭
	Total Float	——
	Free Float	•••••••

13 Managing Risks and Issues

1. Draw a diagram to illustrate the Risk Management process and use it to explain a process for managing threats.

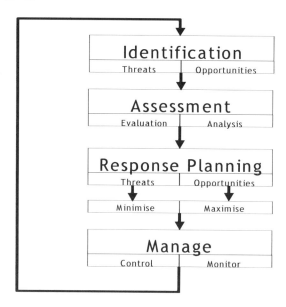

Stage 1 Identification
As many possible threats as possible are identified using such techniques as:

- Brainstorming

- SWOT Analysis
- Assumptions Analysis
- Constraints analysis
- Using the WBS
- Interviews

Stage 2 Assessment

The identified risks must then be assessed and prioritised. This is best done by determining probability and impact and plotting them on a probability & impact grid. This can be done in a Qualitative sense on a 1 to 5 point scale e.g Very Low, Low, Medium, High, and Very High or Quantitatively by using actual values. Risk Exposure is Impact x Probability and this value can be used to prioritise the risks.

Stage 3 Response Planning

An appropriate response must be formulated for each identified risk. There are 5 common strategies for addressing downside risks or threats. These are applied either individually or in combination.

1. Avoid
2. Transfer
3. Reduce/Mitigate
4. Accept
5. Contingency Plan

Stage 4 Manage

Each risk that has a planned response must be proactively managed by the person responsible. In addition the risk plan needs to be formally reviewed on a regular basis.

The situation is bound to change because:-

- Some risks mature into problems (issues)
- Some risks are resolved or do not arise
- Probability/impacts change; up or down
- New risks arise that were not identified initially
- Project scope changes give new risk opportunities

The primary tool for managing risk is the Risk Register

2a. From the grid below identify the top 4 risks. (For grid see question)

Exposure = probability x impact

The top 4 risks are 6, 7, 2, 10 with Exposures 20,20,16,15 respectively

2b State 4 appropriate responses to these risks.

1. **Avoid** the risk and eliminate uncertainty by just not doing it or doing it in a different way
2. **Transfer** liability or ownership of a risk to someone else such as the client or sub-contractor by means of insurance or back to back contracts
3. Take appropriate actions to **Reduce/Mitigate** the risk
4. Prepare a **Contingency Plan** to execute if the risk is triggered.

(note that Acceptance is not an option for high exposure risks)

2c State 4 generic actions that a project manager would take in planning a response to a particular risk.

1. Identify possible responses

2. Evaluate each responses by estimating the cost of mitigation how much the exposure has been reduced

3. Identify the most effective response

4. Check the affect on the budget against the business plan to see if the project is still viable

----

14 Quality Management

1a. Describe the purpose of project quality management.

The purpose of Project Quality Management is to ensure that project processes and outputs meet the requirements of the Quality Plan and thus ensure that the resultant deliverables, meet the specification, are fit for purpose and meet customer requirements.

1b Describe 4 key processes in quality management.

1 Quality Planning

Quality planning is defined as identifying which quality standards are relevant to the project and determining how to apply and satisfy them. In other words, setting standards and how to achieve them. The primary output of the quality planning process is the Project Quality Management Plan. It describes how the project team intends to implement its Quality Policy.

2 Quality Assurance

Quality Assurance is defined as the process of evaluating overall project performance on a regular basis to provide confidence that the project will satisfy the relevant quality standards. It is concerned with validating the consistent use of procedures and standards. It is supported by independent quality reviews and audits.

3 Quality Control

Quality Control involves measuring project products to test if they conform to the relevant standards, as defined in the Quality Plan, and also identifying ways to correct unsatisfactory performance and deviation from specification.

4 Continuous improvement

The process of improving quality by a series of continuous small incremental improvements rather than major changes. The philosophy is that quality comes from continuous minor improvements. It is the responsibility of both workers and management to always be on the look out for ways to improve the quality of the finished product and the processes that produce it.

----

2. Explain how a project manager would ensure the quality requirements are achieved during the project. Make 5 points.

1. Make sure that all project personnel are aware of the need for quality and the required quality standards and that they have received the necessary training and are capable of carrying out the work to the appropriate standard

2. Make sure that there is an approved quality plan detailing all the required quality assurance and control procedures and standards and that all the project team and relevant stakeholders are familiar with the requirements of the plan.

3. Make sure everyone is aware, by means of appropriate training and communication, of their roles & responsibilities for carrying out quality management actions. If necessary appoint a Quality Manager.

4. Carry out monitoring and controlling actions to make sure that the product quality is being adhered to as per the quality plan, and that the outcomes of quality audits are noted and acted upon.

5. Ensure there is an effective change control process in place and communicate regularly throughout the project with client and stakeholders to ensure that the project deliverables continue to be aligned with client requirements.

15 Change Control & Configuration Management

1 Explain a typical change control process, making 5 substantial points.

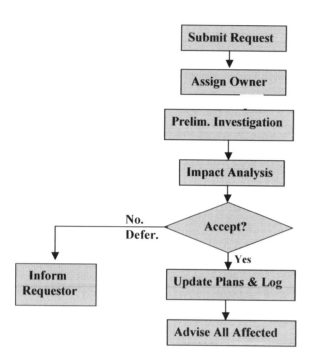

1. Any stakeholder can submit a change request but it must be done in writing using the appropriate documentation. Verbal change requests are not acceptable. An owner will be assigned to manage the processing of the request

2. Even investigating and quantifying a change request can take significant effort so a preliminary investigation will determine if the request should be taken forward.

3. The next step is to appoint someone to carry out a full impact analysis to determine the costs and benefits of the change and the impact on the project plan and the business objectives.

4. A decision to accept, reject or defer the change will be made at an appropriate level. Major changes may require a meeting of the full Change Control Board but lesser changes may be delegated to the project manager or project team members.

5. Whatever the decision, it will be communicated to all relevant parties and if the decision is yes then the change owner will ensure that all plans and documents are updated.
----

2. Define what is meant by Configuration Management and state the 5 principal activities that make up configuration management.

A product is made up of many inter-related components. These include documents such as specifications, designs and plans as well as deliverable components. The totality of items is known as the Configuration. Configuration Management encompasses all the activities concerned with the creation, maintenance and change control of the configuration throughout the project and product life cycle.

1. Configuration Management Planning
  Establishes project specific procedures and defines tools, roles and responsibilities
2. Configuration Identification
  Breaking down the project deliverables into individual configuration items and creating a unique numbering system.
3. Configuration Control
  Maintains version control of all configuration items and the interrelationship between items.
4. Configuration Status Accounting
  Recording of all events that have happened to a system under development to allow comparison with the development plan and to provide traceability.
5. Configuration Audit
  Carried out to demonstrate that the products produced conform to the current specification and all procedures have been followed

----

16 Budgeting, Cost Management & Earned Value

1a. Explain why it is necessary to budget and management costs in a project.

It is necessary to determine a budget for a project in order to ensure that the project is commercially feasible, or if not a commercial project that the costs are acceptable in relation to the planned benefits. The budget must be managed so that costs are known and actions can be taken to control them.

1b. Describe 4 types of cost information needed to manage project cost

1. The budgeted cost and scheduled time of each work package.

This will enable the budget or "S" curve to be plotted which shows planned spending over the planned duration. This is a key control tool and the basis of Earned Value Management.

2. Actual costs and schedule.

For each work package we need to track the actual amount of money spent and when it was spent so we can compare it with the budget.

3. Earned Value.

For each work package we need to measure how much progress has been made. i.e. how much of the task has been completed. Multiplying the budget by the % complete gives the Earned Value.

4. Cost to Complete.

Based on the history to date we can then forecast the final project cost. We can assume that future progress will have the same cost efficiency as that to date or alternatively we can assume that future work will be as per the budgeted plan.

----

2. A project is being monitored using the earned value method, has a budget of £100,000 and is planned to complete in 12 months. The following table shows the situation at the end of month 5.

Month	Planned Value £K	Earned Value £K	Actual Value £K
1	10	5	10
2	20	15	25
3	30	35	40
4	40	40	50
5	50	45	60

At the end of month 5....

a) What are the values of cost variance and schedule variance? State the meaning of these terms.

CV = Earned Value – Actual Value = 45 - 60 = -15 (£K)

By the end of month 5 we have spent £15K more than we planned to spend on the work so far

SV = Earned Value – Planned Value = 45 – 50 = -5 (£K)

By the end of month 5 we are behind schedule by £5K worth of work.

b) What would you estimate the cost at completion to be, making 2 different assumptions about future cost performance?

Assumption 1:- Rest of project continues with same performance.

ECAC = Project Budget/CPI   [CPI = Earned Value/Actual Value = 45/60]

ECAC = 100 x 60/45 = £133,333

Assumption 2:- Rest of project is delivered to plan

ECAC = Project Budget – Cost Variance (CV)

CV = Earned Value – Actual Value = 45 – 60 = -15

ECAC = 100 – (-15) = £115,000

c) What would you estimate the completion time to be, again making 2 different assumptions?

Assumption 1:- Rest of project continues with same performance.

At month 5 Earned Value is 45 against a planned 50. This is half a months' worth of work

Slippage is half a month therefore $SPI_{(time)}$ = 4.5/5 = 0.9

Estimated Completion Time = Original Duration/SPI = 12/.9 = 13.33 Months

Assumption 2:- Rest of project is delivered to plan

Estimated Completion Time = Original Duration + Slippage = 12.5 months.

----

17 Communications & Information Management

1. State 10 practices that a Project Manager should adopt in order to facilitate effective project communication.

1. Have a communications plan and make sure that all relevant stakeholders are familiar with it and comply with it.

2. Always use the most appropriate means when communicating. For instance don't use email when a phone call or face to face is more appropriate

3. Ask for and give feedback. Only by doing this can you be sure that a message has been fully understood.

4. Be available and approachable. You will miss out on much valuable information if you make yourself unapproachable either by just being seen or by your attitude

5. Be aware of blockers and barriers. Many things can interfere with project communications, such as culture, jargon, environment etc. You need to be aware of these factors and take steps to mitigate them.

6. Do not be a communications bottleneck. People need to make decisions when you are not around so although you need to be informed all information does not have to pass through the PM.

7. Hold effective meetings. Meetings need to be properly planned and chaired, and the right people involved. They should have a clear agenda and minutes and actions recorded.

8. Use standard reporting formats. Routine communications will be much more efficient if a standard format is used.

9. Use trigger points and exception reporting. Excessive communication will be reduced if only those variations above agreed trigger points require reporting

10. Keep all stakeholders aware of important events/changes. Make sure they have no surprises

----

2. Explain 5 factors a project manager should consider when developing a communication plan.

1. Information requirements.

The first step is to determine all the project information requirements and the means of acquiring that information. This entails examining the needs of all stakeholders and determining whether that information can be obtained.

2. Data storage and access.

All the information that has been gathered needs to be securely stored. The plan must describe how and where the information must be stored and how it is accessed including access controls

3. Information flow

The means of distributing the information must be determined. What are the communication channels and what is the format, content and level of detail of the information.

4. Communication schedule.

A schedule showing when each type of communication will be produced and to whom it is sent must be developed. This could take the form of a Communication Matrix showing all reports, to whom they are sent and their frequency.

5. Information updating and version control

Information must be kept current so the plan must detail how information is refreshed and updated and how different versions will be controlled.

----

18 Procurement & Negotiation

1. List 5 different contract types/payment structures that you are familiar with and describe for each the situation they would be most appropriate for.

1. Fixed Price/Lump Sum

This approach is best suited for situations where requirements are well defined and costs are predictable. It therefore requires a detailed and unambiguous specification of requirements and agreed acceptance criteria. In this situation the Supplier takes all the majority of risk.

2. Milestone Payment/Planned Payment

This approach is most suitable when a contract can be split into defined stages and/or where stage definition depends on earlier stages. Also suitable when a client does not wish to commit to everything up front. A Total risk to the Supplier is reduced and variations contained within stages

3. Unit Rate Based Payment

This is similar to previous example except pieces of work are very much smaller. It is suitable when the work to be done, or resources required is uncertain at the time of the bid and the client would rather "pay as you go" As the contract is still fixed price the risk is still with the Supplier but less than for the previous examples as the work is in much smaller packages.

4. Cost Reimbursement

This method is most suitable for use when it is unclear at the outset what work will be required and/or it is difficult to quantify. The Supplier is obligated only to make best effort to fulfil the contract within the estimated amount and the buyer funds all overruns. Major risk is now with the Client.

5. Target Cost

This approach is most suitable when entering into partnerships or alliances and the approach is one of shared risk and reward. It can also be a compromise when the supplier is unwilling to take all the risk with a fixed price and the client is unwilling to take on the risk of cost reimbursement.

----

2. List the 5 stages of negotiation and describe the main elements of each stage.

1. Preparation

This is the most important stage. You must decide exactly what you wish to achieve and at what point you will walk away. You need to gather as much information as possible about your opponent especially your relative strengths and weaknesses. You should rehearse the negotiation and try and predict difficult questions. Decide which tactics you might use.

2. Discussion

This is the first face to face stage where the intention is to establish rapport, clarify purpose and agenda, check information and generally form a firm base on which to negotiate

3. Proposition

The Seller will normally state his opening offer or the proposal may be known in which case the buyer may make a counter offer. This then establishes the difference between the two positions and marks the start of the bargaining process.

4. Bargaining

This can often be a lengthy process. To gain agreement, try to link issues e.g if you do this then maybe we could do that. Do not give something for nothing. Do not make a concession without getting something in return. Be aware of the tactics that might be used against you.

5. Agreement

Review and document what has been agreed. Even if you are not formally signing the final contract at that time you must document and sign the agreement reached so there is no possibility of misunderstanding or later retractment.

----

19 Teamwork

1 As a project manager you have inherited an established project team. Explain 5 examples of good practice that you would use to facilitate effective team working.

1. Hold a kick off meeting to formally launch the project and give the team an opportunity to get to know each other. This is particularly important when teams are not co-located. People tend to cooperate better with people they met face to face.

2. Make sure everyone contributes to and "buys in" to the project plan so that they feel ownership of it as a team. People who have had plans imposed on them are more likely to resist them and care less about achieving them.

3. Make sure everyone knows exactly what is expected of them and how their contribution fits into the project goals. People are more motivated if they understand the ultimate objective and how their piece fits in.

4. Understand, support and coach each individual, particularly those that may be feeling less confident. Different people have different needs and although working as a team need to be treated as individuals.

5. Hold regular team building events, preferably outside of the work environment and use them as means to provide motivation, reward and recognition. People need recognition of their contribution to the team. Rewards, if possible, should be tangible.

----

2. Explain the 4 stages a typical team will go through after initial selection
State 3 instances which could cause team development to go backwards

1. Forming
When teams first meet up they may not all know each other. There is confusion, lack of identity and a lack of team purpose and direction. People are anxious because they are not quite sure what their exact role is and how they will fit in with the team.

2. Storming

Some people now start to try and impose their will on the team. Competition will arise for

the best jobs. There may be leadership challenges. Cliques and sub groups may form as people make alliances. Opinions may polarise. There may be a lot of friction.

3. Norming

As roles and responsibilities are agreed and people better understand the project and their contribution then the team starts to settle down. With clear goals to aim for, the team gains confidence and motivation and communicate openly with each other.

4. Performing

The team is now fully functional. People take pride in being a member of the team. They collaborate with each other and trust and support each other. They share responsibility for achieving team goals and function efficiently.

Development could go backwards due to:

- o Changes to team personnel
- o Large scope changes
- o Major setbacks

----

20 Leadership & Conflict Management

1. Describe 5 characteristics of a good leader/project manager

1. They lead by example and are good role models. People should look up to them and aspire to be like them and copy their behaviour. They have integrity.

2. They are excellent communicators. They can communicate with people at all levels and by different means. They can communicate both verbally and in writing, formal and informal. They are good listeners.

3. They are seen to be fair and even handed. They have no favourites and treat everyone equally. They care about their people and are prepared to take risks on their behalf.

4. They are good at the technical aspects of project management. As well as skilful in leading and motivating people they must be excellent at all the basic PM skills such as planning and organising but also expert in techniques such as scheduling and earned value management

5. Will be available and approachable and know what is going on. Project managers cannot be remote from their team. Team members must fee they can approach them if they have problems. A good project manager will get out amongst the team and will always know what is going on

----

2. Explain5 different approaches to managing conflict.

1. Withdrawal

This is the do nothing option. Just ignore the problem. This shows low concern for both the problem and the ongoing relationship and is a lose-lose situation as the conflict still exists.

2. Smoothing

In this situation the parties wish to remain friends and therefore try and smooth over their disagreement by for instance agreeing to differ. This is still lose-lose as the underlying conflict still exists and the problem has not been solved.

3. Compromising

A middle way is found that both parties can accept. Relationships are protected but this is still lose-lose because neither party gets everything they want and must give something up.

4. Forcing

In this situation one party to the conflict has authority over the other and has imposed their preferred solution. From the point of view of the winner the problem has been solved, but at the expense of the relationship. This is a win-lose situation.

5. Confrontation

In this scenario both parties together explore the best solution to the problem i.e. they confront the issue, not each other. During this process one or both parties may change their view but they both agree that the resulting solution is the best and because of this and the fact that the relationship has been maintained, or even enhanced, this is win-win.

----

21 Health, Safety & Environmental Management

1. Explain5 actions required of the project manager on behalf of the employer that must be taken to comply with Health and Safety legislation.
What are the benefits to the organisation?

1. Carry out a Project Risk Assessment

This concerns health and safety risk to personnel and risk to the project. The Employer, or the PM on his behalf, must ensure that all possible sources of risk are identified and appropriate measures taken to eliminate or minimise them.

2. Implement a Health & Safety Policy for the project

There should be a formal written H&S Policy for the project which states how H&S will be managed and implemented and defines roles & responsibilities. The PM must ensure that the policy is implemented

3. Facilitate training and briefing relative to Health & Safety

The PM must ensure that all project personnel receive appropriate H&S training and that measures are in place to ensure the H&S of visitors to the project locations.

4. Provide H&S reporting, review and improvement

The PM must ensure that all H&S activities are recorded and procedures are regularly reviewed and appropriate improvements made.

5. In particular all of the following must be reported to the H&S Executive
- Death or major injury
- Other injuries resulting in more than 3 days absence
- Work related diseases
- Dangerous occurrences (no injury occurs but could have done so)

Benefits
- There will be increased morale of the workforce
- Better industrial relations
- There will be reduced compensation claims
- Reduced probability of prosecution
- Less disruption due to accidents and sick leave
- Improved company image and reputation

2. Explain the overall aim of the Health and Safety at Work Act, 1974).
   List 5 specific duties of care upon employers regarding health and safety at work and 3 specific duties of care upon employees.

Overall aim

The overall aim of the act is to set out general duties of Employers towards Staff and the Public and also between Employees. It defines the employers "duty of care" and also responsibilities of staff to each other and to their own personal safety. It is based on "common sense" and what is reasonably practical.

Employer's duties of care
   1) To provide a safe & suitable work environment
   2) To consider the mental well being of employees
   3) To consider the physical well being
   4) To make sure that there is proper lighting in place appropriate to the work
   5) To allow regular rest periods

Employee's duties of care
   1) To take reasonable care of their own health & safety and that of others who may be affected by their actions
   2) Cooperate with management to meet the employers legal obligations
   3) Not to intentionally or recklessly interfere with or misuse anything provided in the interests of health, safety or welfare

----

22 Handover & Closeout

1. Explain an effective handover process. Make 5 points.

1. Prepare the Handover Plan.

This should be agreed with the Client. It will define all the steps of the handover process, roles and responsibilities and acceptance criteria and any ongoing support and training requirements.

2. Preparation and testing of deliverables by the project team prior to formal handover.

This is to ensure that the handover will go smoothly and that any problems are fixed before involving the client.

3. Carry out acceptance tests with the Client and users.

These tests will be those previously agreed with the client end user representatives. If the tests are passed then acceptance should be automatic

4. Document results of tests and if satisfactory transfer responsibility and formal ownership.

It is important to formally transfer ownership. If the tests are not satisfactory the process may have to be stopped whist remedial actions take place.

5. Agree and document outstanding issues regarding bug fixes/snagging lists.

Even though the deliverables may pass Acceptance there will probably still be minor outstanding issues and there needs to be a plan in place to address them. A portion of the fee may be withheld until they are completed.

----

2. Explain 5 things a project manager should consider when planning the post project review

1. Who will facilitate it?

This should be an independent facilitator and not the project manager or the sponsor. This will ensure that there is no bias and no one is attempting to protect their own position.

2. Who should be present?

Everyone who can contribute should be present without making the numbers excessive. e.g team members, key stakeholders such as end users and important suppliers and contractors.

3. When will it take place?

As soon as possible after project handover whilst people are still around and memories are freshest. Once the project team has disbanded it can be very difficult to get them back together.

4. Who will record the conclusions and lessons learned and produce the report?

Ideally this should be the independent facilitator but the job usually falls to the project manager. A facilitator may be prepared to give up a day to chair a meeting but may not be prepared to take responsibility for producing a report.

5. How will the lessons learned be disseminated?

The whole point of doing a review is to learn lessons and apply them to future projects. If there is no existing procedure for doing this the project manager must devise his own means.
